# FIELD SPORTS IN INDIA

# FIELD SPORTS IN INDIA 1800-1947

Major-General J. G. Elliott

with Two Chapters on PIGSTICKING by
**Brigadier C. R. Templer**
and A FOREWORD by
**Wilson Stephens**

GENTRY BOOKS · LONDON

First published 1973

I.S.B.N. 0 85614 0236


Published by
GENTRY BOOKS LIMITED
17, Southampton Place, London WC1A 2EH
Layout and Design Brian Roll
Printed by WILLIAM CLOWES & SONS LIMITED
London, Beccles and Colchester

To BARBARA

Whose interest and encouragement never failed.

## ACKNOWLEDGMENTS

For permission to quote from books where the copyright is still in force I am indebted to publishers and authors as follows:

Allen & Unwin Ltd; *The Tiger Roars* by Kenneth Anderson. Edward Arnold Ltd; *Wild Animals in Central India* by A. A. Dunbar Brander and *Sport and Folklore in the Himalayas* by H. L. Haughton. William Blackwood and Sons Ltd.; *Sport and Life in the Further Himalaya* by R. L. Kennion and *Sport and Politics under an Eastern Sky* by the Earl of Ronaldshay. The Bodley Head; *Stalks in the Himalayas* by E. P. Stebbing. The Bombay Natural History Society; *Circumventing the Mahseer* by A. StJ. Macdonald and *The Game Birds of India, Burma and Ceylon* by Stuart Baker. Chapman & Hall Ltd.; *Tiger Slayer by Order* by C. E. Gouldsbury. Peter Davies Ltd.; *Pundits and Elephants* by the Earl of Lytton. Jonathan Cape Limited; *The Men who ruled India—The Guardians* by Philip Woodruff. Faber and Faber Ltd.; *The Lonely Tiger* by Hugh Allen and *Call of the Tiger* by M. M. Ismail. Robert Hale & Company; *Tryst with Tigers* Sher Jung. William Heinemann Ltd.; *H.R.H. Prince of Wales's Sporting Tour* by B. C. Ellison. Macmillan; *Cavalry Surgeon* by A. McKenzie Annand and *Hunter's Moon* by Leonard Handley. John Murray; *Forest Life in India* by Hon. J. W. Best. Oxford University Press; *Maneaters of Kumaon* and *The Temple Tiger* by Jim Corbett. Seeley, Service & Co. Ltd.; *Sport and Wild Life in the Deccan* by R. G. Burton. Thacker, Spink & Co. Ltd. *Trout Fishing in Kashmir* by Alban Wilson. H. F. & G. Witherby Ltd.; *In the High Himalayas* by Hugh Whistler. Mrs George Bambridge, Methuen & Co. and the Macmillan Co. of Canada, a verse from *The Feet of the Young Men* taken from *The Five Nations* by Rudyard Kipling.

*Big Game Hunting in the Himalayas and Tibet* by Gerald Burrard, Miss Elizabeth Burrard, and *Call of the Tiger* by Col. A. N. W. Powell, the author.

The illustrations of Modern Pigsticking appear by permission of Fores Ltd.

The quotations from the Royal Artillery Journal are by permission of the Editor and The Hog Hunter's Annual by the kindness of Brigadier J. Scott-Cockburn.

I thank the Librarian and Staff of the India Office Library for their help and for allowing me to reproduce illustrations from their copy of *Oriental Field Sports*. Also the Librarians of the Royal United Service Institute, The Royal Commonwealth Society, The Royal Artillery Institution, The Institution of Royal Engineers, The Fly Fishers Club, and Hardy Bros., Alnwick.

I am deeply indebted to the Editor of *The Field* for allowing me to quote from the records of the magazine dating back to 1852 and for the loan of the photographs that appear as illustrations.

Lt.-Col. F. E. Drake-Briscoe, Brigadier W. E. Gimson, Ralph Morris, Lt.-Col. A. B. L. Peake, Sergt. Mark and Col. H. L. Smith have lent me valuable books and papers.

Finally I thank my friends Charles Frye, Raymond Johnson, Graeme Scotland and Wilfred Whitehead who have dipped into their memories and told me what they found there.

Exmouth
September 1972.

J. G. Elliott

# Contents

# Illustrations



The headings to Chapters Four and Five were drawn by Fergus Kyle and the sheep and goats on page 161 were drawn by Monica Bond.

**MAPS**



The maps on pages 32–33 and 130–131 were drawn by Leo Vernon and are based on 2m sheets published by the Survey of India and made available by the Map Room, India Office Records.

# Foreword

Two things become forgotten about the sport which Britons enjoyed in India. One is the effect it had on the outlook and habits of the British people, not merely on those who served there; the other its effects on the sub-continent's wild life. In this well-documented story, General Elliott traces both themes.

He does so as a past participant, but with a soldier's objectivity. It would have been easy to romanticise over the incomparable atmosphere, background, scenery and companionship. He resists the temptation while giving these aspects their historic weight. But he does not overstep the evidence nor allow his record to become unbalanced.

It would have been easy, too, to adopt by implication an attitude of 'We told you so' in regard to the present sad state of Indian wild life. Species plentiful, some too plentiful, at the time of Partition are now the subject of urgent efforts to prevent their extinction. How did this astonishing reversal happen? General Elliott indicates, but does not blame.

For this he will earn the gratitude of those who know first hand the concept of which he writes. One does not carp about the conduct of friends. Both directly and indirectly there emerges from this account the reality of the immense regard which Britons formed for Indians who shared their sport, and *vice versa*. It became so strong and seemed so natural, as indeed it was, that the Britons came to see India non-possessively as *their* country; and Indians to see the Britons unaffectedly as *their* compatriots.

This relationship broke down when simple communities of interest such as the avoidance of famine and plague, the construction of roads and railways, the sharing of the profession of arms, and last but not least sport, became submerged by the machinations of politicians. Most of these on both sides were London-hatched, remote from the simplicities of the countryside of the immense land for which they felt concern. Though British withdrawal was inevitable, the manner of it was a sorry turn of events which should, and but for the Second World War, would have been better arranged.

To look back in anger is seldom helpful. Better by far to look back in gratitude for good things enjoyed, and to celebrate fraternity even if the brotherhood is past and gone. This is what General Elliott has done.

It is right to stress here one point which he himself makes. This is that big game hunting in India, or small game shooting for that matter, was not a rich man's sport nor did those persons who had prestige and influence dominate it to the disadvantage of others. Generals are not born such; they develop from subalterns. General Elliott, writing retrospectively, makes the point that his own experience of the sport was that of an impecunious junior officer of Indian infantry. This was about as far from prestige and influence as one could get. The point is that as such he had princely pleasure.

Of course wealth helped those who possessed it. Wealth always does. But wealth tends to attach to those of mature years and, while there were many hardy veterans of the forest, the mountain, and even of the *jhow*, young men set the tone. The keynote of *shikar*, that word which is a passport to the magic recreated in this book, was of youth at the peak of anticipation, excitement, participation, achievement, satisfaction. The trophies that remain on the walls—many have disappeared into the attics—are growing a little elderly now. Not so the memories of which they are the expression. They are always young.

If *shikar* is a magic word, it also has practical significance which must not be forgotten. It is Hindi in origin and means simply 'hunting'. It was traditionally the form of hospitality that the Indian of the villages, who had not much to give, offered to those who met him on his home ground. Above all else, *shikar* stood for fair tactics and respect for the quarry. This was the point where the feelings of Indians of the countryside and the chivalries of British sportsmen met and fortified each other.

Two unwritten rules became mandatory. One was that any lapse from sportsmanship was unforgivable, the word soon went round and the offender acquired an unenviable reputation. The other that overkill in the sense of reduction of a species was never risked. The forest block and permit system of conservation produced a higher-than-natural regeneration rate and this was the margin in which sportsmen operated.

As this record shows, it was John Company's young men who

began the tradition of sport in India. By doing so, and in recognition of some thoughtless early excesses, they founded the ethic for sport anywhere. They were setting out in search of tiger, buffalo and sambhur before the 'discovery' of the Highlands by Queen Victoria and her Consort had established stalking there with its rigid code of conduct; before a man could describe himself as a 'rifle', for rifles had not been evolved, and neither had breech-loading. The first men to confront big game did so with muzzle-loading smooth-bores. It was just as well to put the first bullet in a killing spot; just as well too, that the gun should fire. Sometimes it did not.

There are early pictures of the pursuit of carnivorous game with the spear. This was a test of manliness followed in the martial classes and communities, particularly in the princely families. It depended on the quarry charging the hunter, the basic technique being that of the matador. Its chief legacy to the British was the idiosyncratic sport of pigsticking.

To the urban ear in the modern age the term must have unattractive overtones. To the participants it was very much the contrary. No sport ever engaged its devotees more completely. It became both a code of conduct and a way of life for them. To win the Kadir Cup conferred immortality. Attempts to do so fell not far short of pursuit of the Holy Grail.

They were not the unimaginative insensitive sort of men whom the name of the sport might suggest. Most of them could and did let their hair down at a party, singing wild songs and casting care aside. But some were abstemious to a degree. Strangely contrasting names come to mind.

Cavalry officers took naturally to the sport, as might be expected. Two Grenfell brothers, scions of a poetic and philanthropic family, won deathless fame. Robert Baden-Powell, founder of the Boy Scouts, looked back in old age upon the Meerut Tent Club as the valhalla of his youth. But no name figures so often in the list of winners of the Kadir and Muttra Cups as the Royal Regiment of Artillery. The reason is not far to seek. There were always one or more batteries stationed at such famous pigsticking centres as Meerut, Muttra and Jhansi, and the permanency of a Gunner Mess was the foundation on which the local sport was based. When many might have thought them old enough to know better, more than one High Court judge laid aside his wig and risked life and limb in that glorious chase.

Two things characterised them all. First, a regard for the horses they rode second only (and sometimes a close second) to love for their wives; then a ceaseless concern for the *shikari* and the beaters who, on foot and in conditions demanding immense endurance, lent their age-old skill and courage to the organisation of the chase. The 'pig' they faced were not the comfortable, plethoric creatures of farm and sty, but wild boars consisting of two or three hundred-weight of bone, muscle, cunning and aggression, and not an ounce of superfluous flesh.

They and similarly formidable quarry flourished until the last days of the Raj. Not so now. It is best to be as non-accusatory as General Elliott but there is no hiding the fact that restraints, which had been practised by all when paramountcy seemed to guarantee the future, ceased when the last troopship sailed out of Bombay harbour. Some of the motivations are not difficult to understand.

Few ideas are as contagious as each-man-for-himself (don't we know it here?). Take off the brakes, and there is no speed limit when it comes to keeping up with the Joneses, or their opposite numbers. The voice of restraint is generally the voice of experience, and was in fact much raised. But the voice of experience also sounds like the voice of reaction, and 'the square' is as widely recognised and under-valued in modern India as in latter-day Britain. Moreover some of those who, in the security of this and other temperate and developed countries, plead for the conservation of, say, tigers and leopards, might be less eloquent if they found the pug marks of the former at their gates, or heard the latter coughing in the dusk a stone's throw from the village—especially if a stone was all they had to throw.

So a heritage has been largely, but not quite irretrievably squandered. Happy days have been overtaken by that old fugitive, Time. Omar Khayyam, recalling a vanished splendour, said that 'the lion and lizard keep the courts where Jamshyd gloried'. We must hope that, devoid of the paradoxical safeguard of *shikar*, India does not end with only the lizard.

WILSON STEPHENS

*The Field*,
8 Stratton Street,
Piccadilly,
W.1.

# Introduction

Sometime about 1860, his book is not dated, Captain George Francklin Atkinson of the Bengal Engineers wrote a series of satirical sketches which he published under the title of *Curry and Rice, on Forty Plates*, or *The Ingredients of Social Life at 'Our Station'* in India: more specifically in Bengal. He dedicates the work to 'My Dear Thackeray', suggesting that 'his tiny vessel is to follow in the wake of your big men-of-war, the sound of its popguns lost in the crash of your thundering artillery'. In his preface to the reader he allows that the perfect individual affords no scope for the exercise of humour, the word is his own, 'it is only as perfection is deviated from that the victim becomes the object of wit and the shaft of ridicule'. Accordingly it must be realised that 'in singling out the faults and absurdities of our race' his object was to 'afford amusement by dwelling on the sunny side of Indian life after all the narratives of horror that have of late fallen on English ears'.

Satire is all very well so long as the knife is sharp and the reader is familiar with the background against which it is written. Failing that he may be misled into mistaking fiction for fact. *Curry and Rice* is pretty heavy going and the writer seems to be concerned only to paint a picture of a band of exiles who console themselves with a round of trivialities, gossip being their staple diet. The trouble is that so many who came after him, satirists, novelists, and even some who claim to present a considered study of the life of the British in India, never seem to have bothered to ask if there was another side to the picture. 'Duty and red tape, picnics and adultery' was the verdict of a writer in *Vanity Fair*, and they have been content to leave it at that.

There was some truth in the charge, but if that was all there was to life in India how came it that a high place in the civil service examinations or in the passing-out list from Sandhurst, was a *sine qua non* for the young man who hoped to be posted to the Indian Civil Service or commissioned into the Indian Army? The truth is that the Indian Civil offered responsibility far more challenging than a desk-bound job in Whitehall, the Indian Army a life more exciting than the monotonous shuttle between Aldershot and Salisbury Plain.

And for relaxation? *Curry and Rice*'s picture of *Our Station* which appears at the head of Chapter One leaves one in no doubt that some stimulus was needed to offset the monotony of life in such drab surroundings. Something more exciting than picnics. Field sports in India—and there was a wide variety to choose from—offered the necessary relief from the circumscribed social round, whether in cantonments, civil station, or on leave. Over the period of two hundred odd years there were many who sought this relief, and for those who did it became a part of their lives.

The object of this book is not so much to prove what the reader must accept as a statement of fact, as to discover just what the attraction was. And for that one can only try to recapture the charm and underline the contrast with the life from which it was an escape.

I have written inevitably from the angle I know best, that of the ordinary, unprivileged officer of Indian infantry, who had to work for what he got, but I hope it is clear that we were not the only ones. The officers of the British Army, of the Indian Civil Service, the Police, and all the others got as much kick out of it as we did. To say nothing of the men of the Indian Forest Service who gave us every encouragement and, incidentally, were as much concerned with the hunted as with the hunters. If they had had more worthy successors there would be more tigers alive today.

# 1. Shikar as a Part of Life

*'Our Station'*

On 15th August 1947 the Dominions of India and Pakistan, as they were then styled, came into being and the exodus of Britons began in real earnest. Civil servants of all grades, officers and men of the three services, pensioners, who had planned to end their days in the India they had served, arrived in Bombay by mail train and military special in a steady stream. And all their wordly goods came with them. The stacks of luggage mounted on the platforms and were spirited away to the docks under the watchful eye of the old Parsee shipping clerk in the high, shiny hat. There was little, except the labels, by which even their owners could tell one pile from another; neatly patched bedrolls, uniform cases, the names in white paint worn faint by miles of travel, and of course, the gun cases. Canvas-clad and stained with oil they were the poor relations of the portmanteaux in opulent hide to be seen on the platforms of Euston or King's Cross on the eve of The Twelfth. And the guns inside, though reckoned singly and not in pairs, had to their credit bags which made up in variety what they may have lacked in numbers. They were all marked 'Not Wanted on Voyage': some of them would never be wanted again in the hands of those who then owned them. They were part of a way of life, symbols of a passing era.

## FIELD SPORTS IN INDIA

The troops of the Honourable East India Company, fighting their way against the Mahrattas north west from Calcutta to the frontier on the Jumna, found a countryside where the cultivation surrounding the villages was interspersed with areas of thick jungle, tall trees growing out of dense undergrowth and extensive thickets laced with briers. And through this plentiful cover swarmed tiger, pig, deer, peacock, partridge, quail, snipe and duck. Small wonder that the officers of those days turned to sport for relaxation, setting a fashion that persisted to the end. By the start of the nineteenth century field sports were everywhere recognised as part and parcel of the life of the British community. In 1804 the Marquess of Wellesley addressed a cogent minute to the Court of Directors advocating the establishment of a zoo worthy of the teeming fauna of the country. In anticipation of sanction he set up the Barrackpore Menagerie, but the Court, who took a realistic view of the objects on which the Company's money could properly be spent, would have none of it; resisting even the blandishment of a series of paintings of animals and birds, by Dr Buchanan Hamilton and Indian artists working under him, which the Marquess sent home to lend colour to his proposal. These sketches are still on view in the India Office Library.

In 1807 Ormes of Bond Street published Williamson and Howitt's *Oriental Field Sports*. Family album size, the clarity of the text and the charm and vigour of the plates are eloquent testimony to the place that field sports had established for themselves. The plates are titled in French as well as English. There is further evidence in the diary of Lieutenant John Pester for the years 1802–6, *War and Sport in India*, which covers a period of fighting the Mahrattas in the triangle Delhi–Bareilly–Gwalior. John Pester did nothing by halves. On hearing that war with the Mahrattas was inevitable he notes: 'if an officer should wish to get forward he should pray for opportunities to distinguish himself and let none escape that offer. To be first and foremost in danger should be his object. If he falls, he falls gallant and respected, and it is a thousand to one if he is not rewarded should he succeed in doing his duty in the style of a soldier.' And he welcomes the appointment to command his brigade of one Colonel Whyte, who by his gallantry had earned the name of the God of War. When not fighting, Pester was out in search of game, preferably under conditions that involved some risk to life and limb. It was clear that in time of war an officer should not study comfort, but he saw no point in hardship for its own sake. Be as comfortable as you can. 'Packed ten dozen of Madeira and four dozen of port with some beer in grass for the march.' 'Our guns, elephants, servants with a good store of claret, madeira, fowls, hams etc. etc. left cantonments today.'

The officers of those days were born and bred in the English countryside and a love of sport was in the blood. There was game to be ridden, hunted or shot by anyone who took the trouble to ride a mile or two out of camp or cantonment. 'We had agreed to fire at nothing but tiger, and in consequence the deer and hogs, which we found in greater abundance than I could have believed, all escaped.'

Those halcyon days did not last for ever but the next seventy-five years were the era of the great shikaris: Williamson, Shakespeare, Burton, Kinloch, Forsyth, Gordon, Cumming, Sanderson, Baker, Pollock, to name but a few of them. Game was everywhere plentiful and there was little limit or restriction imposed on what they shot, or where. In fact it was a matter of government policy to clear whole areas of game to open up fresh tracts for cultivation. About 1880 it began to dawn on the early conservationists that things had gone far enough. Soil erosion, following in the footsteps of the sacred cow, was stripping the countryside bare up to the boundaries of the government forests. And inside those forests some control became necessary over what might be shot. The early game laws date from then. Responsibility for giving effect to these laws rested with the officers of the Indian Forest Service, men who spent the months from November to March in the jungle, 'wise in more than wood-lore alone', and they made a good job of it.

With the tradition of the English hunting field behind them the early sportsmen very soon took pigsticking to their hearts. Using its own distinctive weapon pigsticking has always remained in a class of its own. After one or two experiments the long spear, which came into use about 1840, remained in use unchanged over the next hundred years; and so did the methods of using it. Nothing could be simpler or more direct. The sport had a respectable ancestry. Ovid, in the eighth book of Metamorphoses, describes a boar hunt in 1400 B.C. when Atalanta was awarded the skin and tushes. In the Ajanta caves near Bombay there is a painting of a scene three thousand years later that shows mounted men pursuing a boar, and in the Lahore Museum there is a spirited picture dated about 1690 of a Rajput warrior complete with bow and arrows engaging a charging boar with a sword.

At the time of the First World War field sports were still firmly established in favour and, if one can believe the evidence of an India Office letter circulated in 1916, they were within the reach of everyone. At that time the Indian Army had suffered heavy casualties in France and Mesopotamia and there was an urgent need for men with battle experience to officer the wartime battalions that were being raised. The obvious recruiting ground was among officers of the British Army who had fought in France. Deciding that if it was to be done it must be done well, an offer was made of permanent commissions in the post-war army. No pains were spared to paint the prospects in glowing terms. The task was given to one Colonel Ramsay Gordon and it is clear that he wrote from the heart. The letter which bears his signature earned the flippant sub-title of 'Tigers at the bottom of the Compound'. It began with a few sordid details about pay and pensions, and had a word to say for the attraction for the serious soldier of small wars on the frontier, but after that, the ink warm and flowing freely, the writer really gets down to it. The rest of the letter is required reading for every travel agent. 'Apart from soldiering, India offers attractions in the way of games and sport which cannot be beaten anywhere. Big and small game shooting such as, in Europe, is open only to the very rich, in India is within reach of all.' 'Pigsticking, of which India has practically a monopoly, is the King of sports, but not the sport of Kings, as the most impecunious subaltern can join in.' 'Fishing for mahseer affords splendid sport. The rivers, with very few exceptions, are open to everyone and fish up to 50 and 60 lb are frequently to be caught, amidst surroundings and scenery which make Scotland seem tame.' 'The summer heat is no doubt unpleasant but, on the other hand, most of the fishing and big game shooting occurs during the hot weather.' 'Kashmir, which is now only a few hours by motor from the Plains, provides fishing and big game shooting of a very high order and thus adds considerably to the possibilities of sport and pleasure, in a delightful climate during the summer months.' 'For the keen soldier India is a land of many opportunities, and for the keen sportsman, of moderate means, a paradise.'

Between three and four hundred officers took the fly floated so skilfully over their noses.

And what of the Promised Land? Did it live up to expectations? The letter was a bit overdrawn, but substantially there was a lot of truth in it. Sport was there for those with a mind to look for it, and many of those coming out to India to the I.C.S., the Police and the Army were so minded.

Except for those who hobnobbed with princes and governors, and they had to do little more than take their places in the battue and discharge their firearms at the appropriate moment, the charm of sport in India lay in the depth of the background. From start to finish it was your show. You were pitting your wits against a wild animal, and if you were successful satisfaction came not from having shot it but from the knowledge that you had outwitted it. If you failed it was probably your fault, and you did not make the same mistake again. You had to be very fit and, to cap it all, there could be the spice of danger, that slight tautening of the nerves, the knowledge that when you came to fire you could not afford to miss.

Babur, when he invaded India, had to penetrate no deeper than the banks of the Indus to indulge his favourite sport of hunting rhinoceros. Four hundred years later the soldier in the Punjab or on the North West Frontier in search of big game had to travel to the government forests of the United Provinces or Central Provinces, or even further to the jungles south of Belgaum or down to the Mysore ditch below the Nilgiris. But he got two months leave every year, and that was long enough even to march a hundred miles or more into the mountains behind Kashmir and still have four weeks left for shooting.

The trips taken on long leave are unforgettable. You booked your forest block weeks, even months, ahead, wrote to the Survey of India for large scale maps, and pored over them in anticipation till you felt you knew every corner of them. Then the day came and you were away, away from the heat and dust of the plains, away from the monotony of an individual training programme that decreed that on the first of April each year the trained soldier once more became a recruit, away to the cool and peace of the jungle where you could not walk a hundred yards without seeing a track or hearing a sound that excited your curiosity and tested your jungle lore. Or if your fancy took you into the hills, you marched for a week or ten days through scenery which in truth 'made even Scotland seem tame'. Cold sparkling air; perhaps by the side of the road a tiny waterfall pouring down over a cliff, the rocks tinged with rust, the water, ice cold, tasting faintly of iron; the camp fire outside the tent in the evenings. You stalked barasingh, or ibex or markhor at a height of over 15,000 feet across ground so precipitous you began to wonder why you had ever been fool enough to leave the flat. If you went back empty handed, though you seldom did, you had a host of memories to console you in your disappointment.

If your regiment was stationed in central India, Cawnpore, Jubbulpore, Mhow, Belgaum, the jungle was at your doorstep and if you had your scouts out, and an indulgent colonel who asked no questions if you disappeared for a couple of nights, you might bring back a panther or even a tiger.

But there were few stations where there was not bird shooting and perhaps fishing to be had within a radius of twenty-five miles. When a battalion was due for a change of station and the day drew near for the publication of the Indian Army Order promulgating the moves for the next trooping season, keen students of form would be busy with their forecasts. Coloured largely by the preference of the individual, they were usually wrong. One commanding officer fell heavily in the popularity stakes when word went round that he had been pulling strings in Simla to secure a move to Hyderabad, Sind. Whatever the merits of a hot, dry climate in the eyes of one who was later to be crippled with rheumatism, Hyderabad was a one battalion station, a hundred miles from anywhere, and with an evil reputation for the longest and harshest hot weather in the land. His rating improved slightly, at any rate among the bachelors, when someone pointed out that there was, within easy reach, some of the best duck shooting in the world. As it turned out the battalion was sent to Waziristan, which shows that it does not pay to pull strings.

A great feature was that it was always considered quite natural that you should combine business with pleasure. It was not that duty was neglected, far from it, but if the path of duty led where you might expect to find something to shoot, it was foolish not to go prepared to spend such spare time as there might be as agreeably as possible. It is likely that this custom dates back to the days when all regiments and batteries moving in relief went by march route along the Grand Trunk Road, which had been built for that purpose. When, in 1862, Major Francis of the Bengal Horse Artillery took his battery from Delhi to Hazaribad, two hundred miles north west of Calcutta, they were fifty-six days on the road. This was a large slice out of life, so he took his life with him.

> 'Our party was—self, wife and three children, Dr Francis, Captain Hawkins, Lts. Murray, Graham and Swinton. We formed a family mess. At the first trumpet, about three or four a.m., I slipped on my clothes, wife the same, and in about twenty minutes the carriage came, into which Nellie got with the two children fast asleep, wrapped up in their bedclothes, and started away. About half way, just as it was sunrise, Nellie stopped the carriage and there would be a cart with tea, coffee cake and bread and butter and hot coffee and biscuits for the men. The children were then put back in their carriage with the ayah (nurse) and Nellie would get on her riding horse and accompany me at the head of the battery.'

Camping grounds were seldom more than fourteen miles apart so by noon tents would have been pitched, horses and men watered and fed and in the afternoon 'we contrived to get some shooting'.

## SHIKAR AS A PART OF LIFE

It may be seen from the jacket of this book that they did not always have to wait till they reached camp to enjoy a little sport. As the text explains, most officers would have a man riding behind them with a spear in readiness for just such an encounter. It adds that 'the best time for hunting wolves is on the line of march'. Small wonder then that the Indian Army officer would take his twelve bore to war with him. Despite stringent restrictions on the weight of kit carried, a number of officers took their guns to Lhasa in 1904; and in Mesopotamia in 1917, when the thermometer soared to 120° for weeks on end, two front line battalions could always turn out half a dozen guns to shoot sandgrouse on a Sunday morning: one of them armed with the 'mess gun'.

It would be quite wrong to suppose that these diversions were the preserve of the martial classes: very much the reverse. District officers of the Indian Civil in the cold weather spent weeks, if not months, in camp and if they were so inclined they had remarkable opportunities for combining sport with duty, the one in no way distracting from the proper discharge of the other. There was one commissioner for the Kumaon who took his whole establishment with him into the jungle and arranged his day's work to suit the habits of the tiger, with the result that he did his office work between three and five in the morning, much to the disgust of his clerks who were nothing if not family men. Lady Lawrence in *Indian Embers* gives a picture of her husband, commissioner of Belgaum, 'in shabby shikar clothes at the door of his tent', interviewing village officials and petitioners whose troubles he probably sorted out in ten minutes when he visited the spot the following day. It was the same Henry Lawrence who found himself in the awkward predicament of having to follow up and shoot a wounded tiger in time to catch a train to take him to a meeting of the Legislative Council in Bombay. Luckily the mail train was two hours late, but even so it was a close thing. A far cry from the cloistered calm of Whitehall, black coats and pinstripe trousers, where the worst dilemma to vex a man in a twelve-month might be to double date himself on a brace of committees.

The career of John Pester proves that a man could be a keen sportsman without in any way detracting from his devotion to duty in time of war: indeed the successful shikari was exercising many of the faculties needed by the good soldier in action. There was a commanding officer who saw fit to write in the confidential report of one of his company commanders: 'If he took as much interest in his profession as he does in shikar he would be a good officer.' The victim of course took this as a tremendous compliment, and his record when war came confirms that he trod in the redoubtable Pester's footsteps. He writes:

> 'I think the most exciting and really satisfying shoot I enjoyed was not when the duck got up at Cherand, but when an Iti column supported by two light tanks rushed in a counter-attack on Tumar West Camp (Sidi Barrani) which we had just taken. They jumped from their troop carriers in front of battalion headquarters and R. and I and some four or five signallers and runners got our rifle barrels hot before they decided it was better to put up their hands—and we had the lot in the bag, including the light tanks.'

And what of the wives? In an album in the India Office library there is a photo of a springless horse-drawn vehicle, 'something between a large bathing machine and a very small second class carriage', standing in the middle of a dry, stony river bed. The caption reads 'Mrs W. in tonga'. And there was the forest officer who dedicated a book to his wife, 'who regardless of her own preferences has shared her husband's exile, cheerfully bearing discomforts and inconvenience for his sake'. They did not all find it heavy going. Many who chose to follow the drum did so because they shared their husband's tastes and enjoyed sport as much as he did. They had little patience with the social round and welcomed any chance to get away from it.

It used to be said that in England no man, if he could help it, spent Christmas anywhere but in his own home; in India no one in his senses spent it in cantonments. The Christmas camp was a distinctive feature of British life, and they came all shapes and sizes. Just a couple of bachelors on their own, or the more ambitious occasions when the wives came too. Freedom and informality were the keynote. By general consent the shackles of etiquette and precedence were left behind and commissioner and newly joined subaltern met on equal terms. The host might be a district or forest officer, or a senior policeman, men who spent in the cold weather much of their working lives in camp and commanded the resources to make the occasion a success.

It was by no means a matter of 'picnics and adultery'; sport was seldom anything but hard work. Chukor in the Kurram, or snipe in Malabar, you got your bag in the sweat of your brow. North or south the pattern was much the same. The night in a canal bungalow, or by the side of the jheel under the stars, the start while it was still dark, the first cool, clear hour after dawn, then a hard slog under a punishing sun. You might make a trip down the Indus in a country craft, tying up by night, and shooting across country by day to meet the boat at the next halting place. 'The enjoyment lies in the variety, and if a bag however small ranges from a crocodile to quail, and includes geese, snipe and bustard, there must be few who can resist its charms.'

Small wonder that the memories that survive the years are not primarily concerned with the urge to rush out and kill something. There will be the occasional lucky shot, 'the thrill of a left and right at two geese flying over a peepul tree against a bright blue sky', but far more one remembers the tremendous fascination and spell of the Indian countryside, be it mountain or stream, particularly perhaps the streams. The teeming life and noises of the jungle, The sounds, the rattle of stones under your feet as you panted after chukor on a barren hillside; the smells, as you pulled a foot out of the squelching mud of a snipe jheel.

Even more memorable is the companionship, of wife or brother officer. Or, to go one further, of your orderly, whom you got to know so much better when the bonds of regimental discipline were relaxed. Your shikari, the jungle dwellers who knew so much more about it than you did; the villagers who turned out to beat for you. 'The real Indian,' to quote Jim Corbett, 'the Indian whose loyalty and devotion alone made it possible for a handful of men to administer for close on two hundred years, a vast sub-continent with its teeming millions.'

# 2. The Mighty Nimrods

*Howdah Shooting in the Terai*

Nimrod was 'a mighty hunter before the Lord', and under that pen name a number of articles appeared in sporting magazines at the end of the eighteenth century. Sportsmen later adopted him as their patron. Those who sought their fortunes in India found a country teeming with game, and when the merchants of the Honourable East India Company travelled inland in search of trade they took their guns and rifles with them. Following the example, or more probably setting it, went the officers of the armies they raised to deal with the French, or with native princes misguided enough to trade or intrigue with them.

Extensive areas were still covered with thick jungle, and where there was jungle they found something to hunt or shoot. The main big game areas, most of which survived as such down to 1947, are shown on the map on pages thirty-two–thirty-three. The merchants from Madras found little but snipe in the rice fields that extend for hundreds of miles inland from the capital, but it was a different story when they reached the Nilgiris and moved north into Mysore (Area A). There they found heavy virgin forests, inhabited by a few wild jungle tribes, the stamping ground of elephants, bison and sambhur. Between these tracts and the open, cultivated country was a belt of lighter forest, small timber and bamboos, the home of tiger, panther, cheetal and pig; while in the scrub jungle bordering the cultivation lived bears, ravine deer, wolves and the occasional black buck.

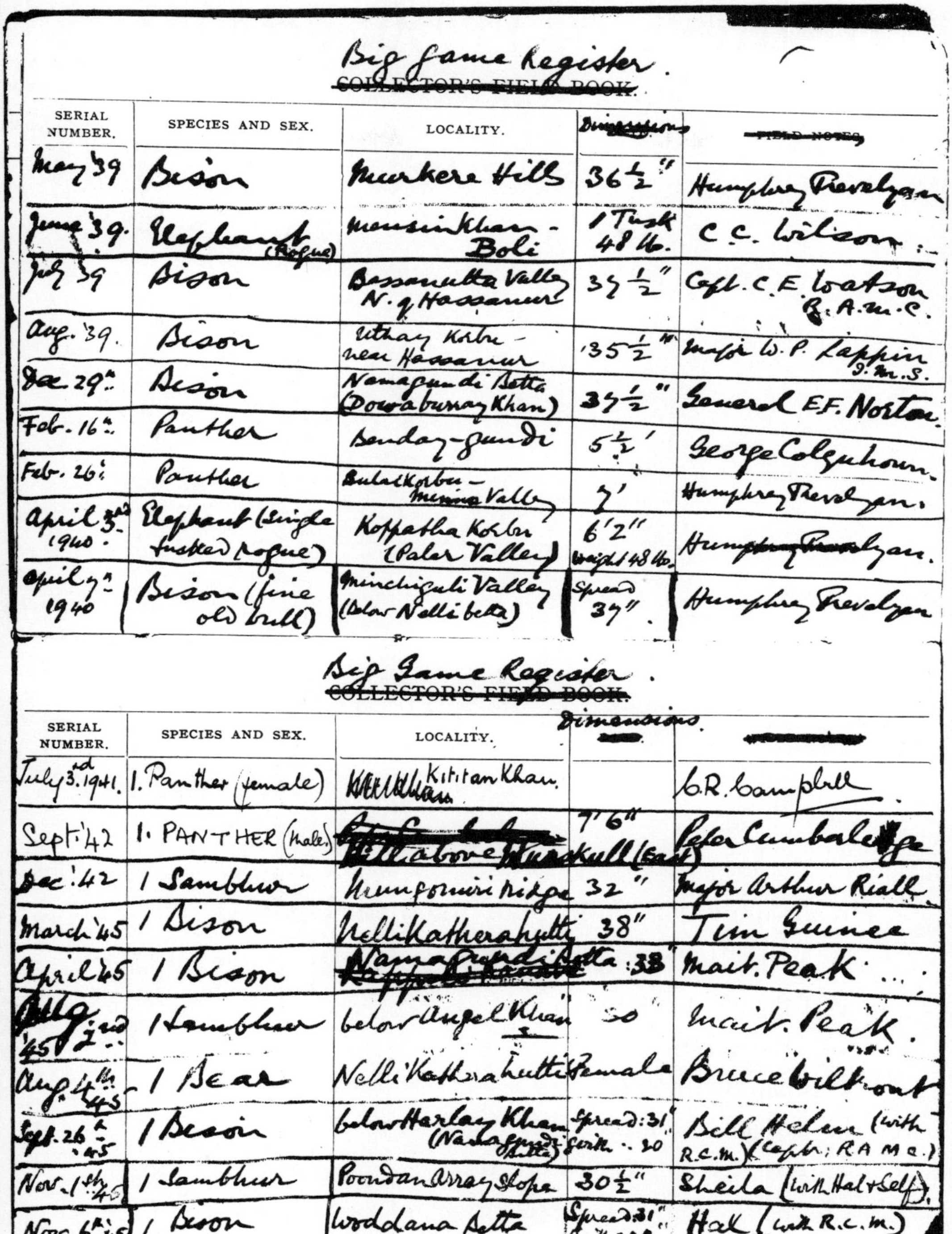

Big Game Register.
~~COLLECTOR'S FIELD BOOK.~~

| SERIAL NUMBER. | SPECIES AND SEX. | LOCALITY. | Dimensions | ~~FIELD NOTES.~~ |
|---|---|---|---|---|
| May '39 | Bison | Murkere Hills | 36½" | Humphrey Trevelyan |
| June '39. | Elephant (Rogue) | Mensinkhan - Boli | 1 Tusk 48 lb. | C. C. Wilson. |
| July '39 | Bison | Bassanutta Valley N. of Hassanur | 37½" | Capt. C. E. Watson R.A.M.C. |
| Aug. '39. | Bison | Uthay Korbe - near Hassanur | 35½" | Major W. P. Lappin I.M.S. |
| Dec. 29th | Bison | Namagundi Betta (Dowabunay Khan) | 37½" | General E.F. Norton |
| Feb. 16th | Panther | Benday-gundi | 5½' | George Colquhoun |
| Feb. 26th | Panther | Bulal Korbe - Menina Valley | 7' | Humphrey Trevelyan. |
| April 3rd 1940. | Elephant (single tusked rogue) | Koppatha Korbe (Palar Valley) | 6'2" weight 48 lb. | Humphrey Trevelyan. |
| April 7th 1940 | Bison (fine old bull) | Minchiguli Valley (below Nelli betta) | Spread 37". | Humphrey Trevelyan |

Big Game Register.
~~COLLECTOR'S FIELD BOOK.~~

| SERIAL NUMBER. | SPECIES AND SEX. | LOCALITY. | Dimensions. | |
|---|---|---|---|---|
| July 3rd 1941. | 1. Panther (female) | Kititan Khan. | | C.R. Campbell |
| Sept. '42 | 1. PANTHER (male) | above | 7'6" skull | Peter Cumberlege |
| Dec. '42 | 1 Sambhur | Mungormiri Ridge | 32" | Major Arthur Riall |
| March '45 | 1 Bison | Nellikatherahutty | 38" | Tim Guinee |
| April '45 | 1 Bison | Namagundi Betta | 38" | Mait. Peak |
| Aug 2nd '45 | 1 Sambhur | below Angel Khan | 30" | Mait. Peak. |
| Aug 4th '45 | 1 Bear | Nelli Katherahutti | female | Bruce Wilmont |
| Sept. 26th '45 | 1 Bison | below Harlay Khan (Namagundi Betta) | Spread: 31" Girth 20" | Bill Helen (with R.C.M.) (Captn. RAMC) |
| Nov. 1st '45 | 1 Sambhur | Poondan Array Slope | 30½" | Sheila (with Hal & Self). |
| Nov. 6th '45 | 1 Bison | Woddana Betta | Spread: 31" Girth 20" | Hal. (with R.C.M.) |

*Planter's Game Register*

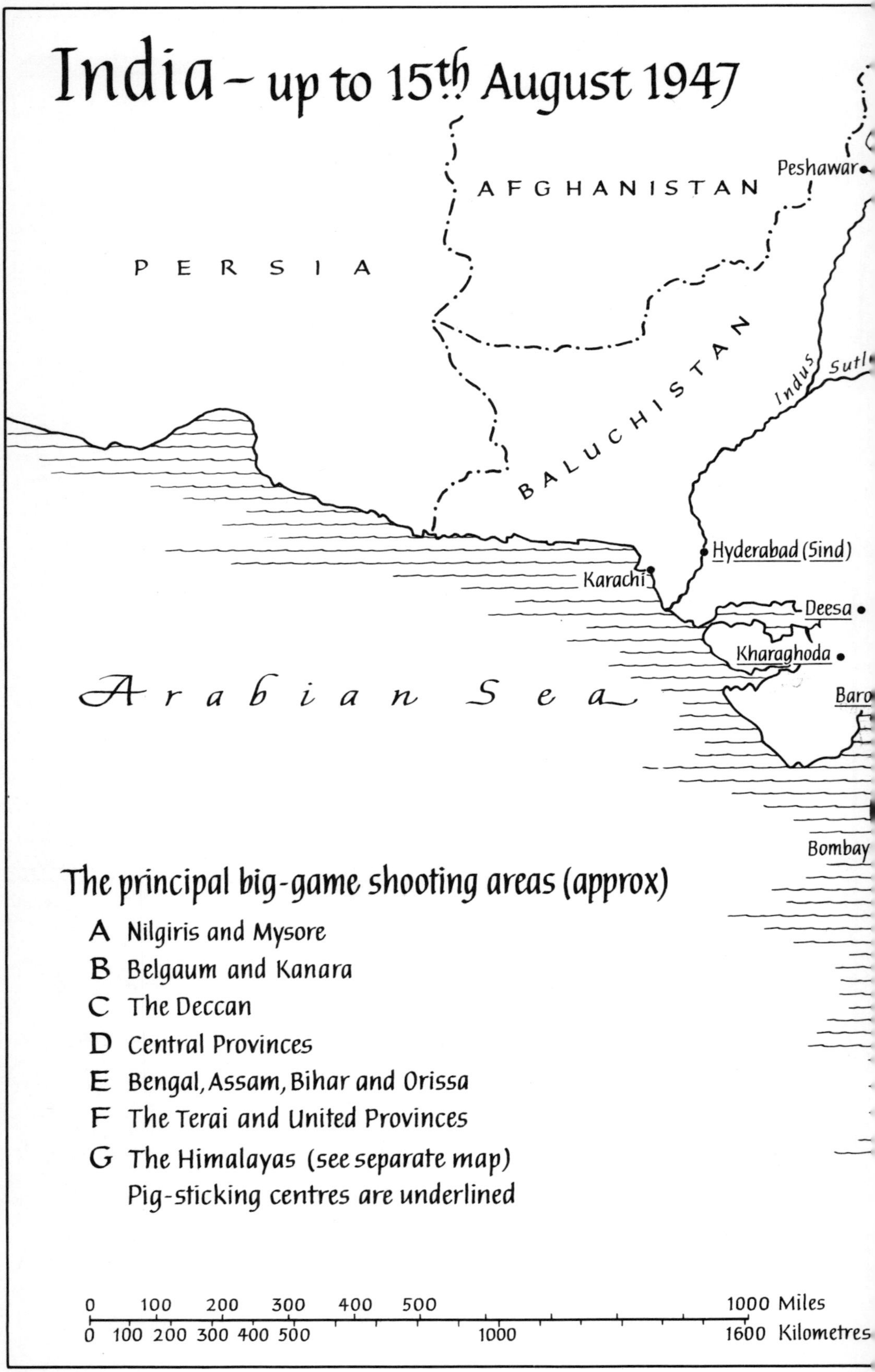
India – up to 15th August 1947
AFGHANISTAN
PERSIA
Peshawar
BALUCHISTAN
Indus
Sutl
Hyderabad (Sind)
Karachi
Deesa
Kharaghoda
Baro
Arabian Sea
Bombay
The principal big-game shooting areas (approx)
A Nilgiris and Mysore
B Belgaum and Kanara
C The Deccan
D Central Provinces
E Bengal, Assam, Bihar and Orissa
F The Terai and United Provinces
G The Himalayas (see separate map)
Pig-sticking centres are underlined
0 100 200 300 400 500 1000 Miles
0 100 200 300 400 500 1000 1600 Kilometres

TIBET
G
walpindi
Lahore
Simla
ozepore
Ambala
Patiala
Dehra Dun
Roorkee
Meerut
Delhi
Moradabad
Bareilly
Budaon
Muttra
Agra
Ganges
Gumti
Jumna
sirabad
Gwalior
Cawnpore
Jhansi
Allahabad
Benares
aipur
NEPAL
F
Tsangpo (Brahmaputra)
BHUTAN
Brahmaputra
ASSAM
Fyzabad
Gogra
Chapra
Patna
Ghazipur
Hazaribagh
BIHAR
Ganges
Paksee
E
BENGAL
Calcutta
Midnapore
BURMA
Saugor
nedabad
Jubbulpore
Mhow
ada
D
Nagpur
ORISSA
Ahmednagar
C
Berhampore
Secunderabad
Bay of Bengal
Belgaum
N
A
Bangalore
Madras
Mysore
Cubbany
leov

There was plenty of game in these jungles right up to 1947, but in the present century, when the bulk of the army moved away to the North West Frontier and the Punjab, it was a far cry for anyone going on leave to travel so far south. Those who did were well rewarded. One planter, Mr R. C. Morris of the Honnametti Estate in Mysore, kept a separate game register to record the trophies shot by his guests, and the extract reproduced on page thirty-one shows what sport he was able to offer them.

The sportsmen from Bombay had to travel no further than Poona or Ahmednagar before they found plenty to interest them. They then had a choice: to the south the jungles of Kanara and Belgaum (Area B), or to the east the Deccan, extending towards Secunderabad (Area C). Bison, tiger and panther were all plentiful.

The men from Bengal were responsible for discovering and opening up the jungles of the Central and United Provinces, which in the present century were the most popular of all. West of Orissa, over the watershed where the rivers start to flow into the Indian Ocean, stand the highlands of Central India (Area D). It was a land of extensive forests of teak and sal, of mineral wealth, with huge tracts of unreclaimed waste and a scanty, half wild population.

> 'A region where all was chaos to the unguided traveller; where hill after hill of the same wild, undefined character are piled together; where the streams seem to run in all directions at once.'

The jungles held tiger, panther, bison, sambhur, cheetal, swamp deer, bear and pig. From April to June when the monsoon broke, it was almost unbearably dry and hot, but sport was so good that the harshness of the climate never stopped anyone going there.

From its foundation, the merchants of Fort St George, Calcutta, were the masterminds in extending the affairs of the Company to the north west, and their sportsmen were the luckiest of them all. They found game at their back door, and across the whole expanse of Area E, including the hill tracts of Chittagong and Assam, both famous for their elephants.

In the Sunderbands, the vast delta of the Ganges, game was plentiful—tiger, deer, hog, rhinoceros and buffalo, but there the sportsmen travelled by boat, not on foot or on elephants, and stalking was difficult if not impossible because of the denseness of the reeds and thickets; to say nothing of the danger from tigers who were the most fearless and confirmed man-eaters in all India.

The jungles of the United Provinces started about Dehra Dun and carried on along the foothills of the Himalayas beyond the provincial boundary for a total of six hundred miles. This is the Terai (Area F). In the south, along the frontier with Nepal, are vast swamps, the last remaining haunt in India of the rhinoceros. The northern half is drier but it is cut by foaming rivers pouring down from their sources in glaciers above the snow line.

The greater part of this immense area consists of forest, dense thicket and tangled vegetation, and where there is water, a very high feathery-tipped grass, appropriately named elephant grass, grows abundantly. Where the grass has been burnt by villagers to obtain fresh pastures for their cattle, park-like glades, clothed in bright green, prevail. And to complete this game reserve, perhaps one of the finest in the world, there are numerous jheels and swamps. It harboured a few elephants, which were strictly preserved, as well as tiger, panther, sambhur and cheetal, barking deer and pig. The heat was never oppressive right up to June, and to fill the cup of happiness you might from your tent or forest bungalow hear one of the snow-fed rivers tearing over rapids into deep pools that were the home of crocodile and turtle. The tiger claimed your attention in the early mornings and evenings, but the forenoon was given over to the mahseer. A six-pounder caught in heavy water on a one-inch fly spoon and a trout rod fought with a fury matched by few other fish.

North of Dehra Dun, the foothills of the Himalayas rise more steeply from the plain and you come to Simla, Kulu and Jammu, behind them to Lahoul, Chamba and the vale of Kashmir; and beyond again to Ladakh, Balistan, Gilgit and Chitral (Area G and map on pp. 130–131). Following the old trade route a handful of the more enterprising penetrated as far as Leh, the capital of Ladakh, as early as the 1860s but this tremendous expanse, where you sought your game at heights ranging from 10,000 to 20,000 feet did not become generally popular until twenty years later.

There are three well-defined though overlapping periods in the story of the sport of the British in India: up to about 1840, for forty years to 1880, and from then to 1947. There was little finesse about it to start with. Few knew or cared much about jungle lore; they were fearless, hard hitting, straightforward Nimrods, ready to ride down with spear or rifle anything they came across. They set the fashion and laid the foundations for those who came after them, but over the next seventy-five years the whole pattern of life changed so much that it is worth a couple of chapters to take a look at what went on in those early carefree days.

## FIELD SPORTS IN INDIA

Major Francis of the Bengal Horse Artillery, who is mentioned in the last chapter, left some notes on his life in India. He fought in the second Sikh War in 1849, and after two years at home on medical certificate, went back to take part in the fighting after the Mutiny. With one more spell of leave he was in India until 1873. His notes constantly refer to sport:

> 'My brother sub. was Dick Mecham. We served together in the same troop for seven years. We had great sport together. Both of us were excellent horsemen; hunting, coursing and pig-sticking we were always ready for. Thousands of miles we have ridden side by side.
>
> 'In the cold season I obtained eighteen days leave and Captain Simeon and I started to shoot along the banks of the canal. I took Nellie with me, and a very enjoyable time we had—first rate snipe and duck shooting, and the pea-fowl were the best I ever ate. Simeon and I used to start after our cups of chocolate and a pipe. Nellie had the carriage into which she put breakfast, and she was told to go from six to eight miles and then get breakfast ready. We shot right away, and making a slight circle round generally hit off the spot, and found the kettle boiling, and we made a hearty gipsy breakfast.
>
> 'I had no time excepting the weekly holiday to go out, and this was on a Saturday. We finally started about four a.m. and got home again about five p.m., riding from 13 to 30 miles, and shooting all day, or if it was a tent club meet, hog hunting for some four hours. My whist club used to dine with me every Saturday; we always broke up at eleven at night. Dinner was at six, a quiet repast with a glass of sherry and beer, and after dinner, with the kettle on the hob, a glass or two of toddy with our cigars.'

It is significant that the years Francis spent in India bracket the period that Atkinson wrote about in *Curry and Rice* when, he would have you believe, life was one long frivolous social round. The key-note of the true picture is surely the simplicity of it all. They worked hard for what they got, and they did not make a fuss about it.

To consider in rather more detail how they set to work, the operative word to describe their activities was not shooting: they hunted. In England it was the heyday of fox hunting and most of the officers coming out to join the Presidency Armies, and many of the civilians, arrived with that background behind them. When they got to India they were agreeably surprised to find that wherever they went there was something for them to shoot or hunt: in particular the pig, an altogether more formidable opponent than the fox, but just as plentiful as rabbits in the English countryside they had left behind them. They set to and hunted him with the spear, and a very exciting sport it was, ranking above any other in the world in the demands it made on nerve and horsemanship. There was in England an unwritten law that protected the fox from being shot: in India, except in heavy jungle where he could not be ridden, they paid the pig the same compliment.

In Chapter 4 there are stories of hog hunters who took a spear to game larger and more dangerous than the old grey boar, and it is clear that the widespread popularity of pigsticking influenced the approach to the pursuit of game of all kinds. The early Nimrods mounted their horses and they hunted their game, though not necessarily with a spear. They rode after it, drew alongside and shot it; and they trained their horses to become accustomed to a rifle being fired off by the rider. In *Seonee* Sterndale describes how they set about it:

> 'Over the swell of the ground at the head of the valley dashes a noble blue bull. A few yards behind pressed a sportsman at the same reckless pace. As the crest of the hill was passed the rider, pressing his horse's flanks, urged him to a final rush, and ranging up alongside the bull, the sharp crack of a rifle rang through the stillness of the glen. Another sharp report and he plunged heavily on his head.
>
> 'The first glance the hunter gave the dying bull was one of mingled satisfaction and pity; his eyes flashed with pride at the well-placed shots, but a sadder expression came over them as they met the glazing orbs of the animal.
>
> '"Poor brute!" he said softly to himself, "you had a sharp tussle for it; but I gave you every chance. I might have shot you down standing where we first came upon you, but I gave you a run for your life."'

Game swarmed over the countryside and village life over large areas was disrupted by man-eaters. When the new military road was built from Calcutta to Benares to cut the distance of the old route along the Ganges, a belt of jungle had to be kept clear for a hundred yards on either side; otherwise tigers would have taken such toll of the travellers that only formed bodies of troops could have used the road. The evolutions of a battalion at drill might be thrown into disorder by a stag seeking refuge from a tiger lurking in the jungle that bordered the parade ground. And when the day's work was over three or four officers would make up a party and go questing after tiger, pig, deer or whatever the countryside offered, much as their successors a hundred years later would go out after partridge or peacock from battalion camp.

The sportsmen of the early days were not above bird shooting for the pot, but they did not have a very high opinion of it as sport. In *The Old Forest Ranger*, Campbell tells how a party of nine set out in the Nilgiris to shoot or spear tiger, pig, deer or bear, whatever they came across. Mounted on sure-footed ponies, they were armed with spears and rifles, and at their heels were half a dozen formidable hounds, a cross between a fox hound and a local breed that resembled a bull dog. The leader of the party was a crusty old gentleman who had very definite views as to what constituted sport and regarded his nephew, who was one of the party, with some misgiving. He certainly had some grounds for doing so for the young man turned out in a glossy hat, fashionably cut green coat, smart hunting kit with tops and white breeches. He suspected him of being addicted to 'the innocent pastime of peacock and jungle fowl shooting, a young gentleman who having devoted his early life to the rearing of tame rabbits has never learned to appreciate the beauties of a grooved barrel'. He addresses him in affectionate terms:

> 'You misbegotten whelp! Do you take me for one of those thistle-whipping vermin who prowl about the woods with a smooth-bore pop gun?'

But under that crusty exterior there ran a sentimental streak, for he was once heard to remark that the thud of his bullet striking a sambhur stag 'was as welcome to a man's ear as the voice of her he loves'.

When game was everywhere so plentiful it is not surprising to read of bags that far exceed in numbers anything that a sportsman of later days would have felt justified in shooting. In *Sport in Bengal*, Baker tells how from his camp, without using his binoculars, he could distinguish 'at least three score wild buffaloes and between two and three hundred spotted deer feeding in the open'.

There were in those days 'two giant Nimrods', one of them Colonel S——d, who shot eleven black buck in a day, the other 'Gunga' Brown who over and over again shot seventy brace and upwards of painted partridge. A party of three guns returned from a ten day shoot with a bag of four tigers, two bears, seven sambhur, two cheetal, one four horned antelope, one hyena, four black buck, four chinkara, two boar, a total of twenty-seven head. This was described as 'very fair sport'.

Before condemning these figures out of hand as sheer butchery it is well to remember the standards of the days in which these men lived. In the span covered by this book there was still a gallows at Tyburn, and no doubt the grandfathers of the men who campaigned for the abolition of capital punishment joined the crowd that went along to see the fun when a notorious malefactor was to be hanged. In 1814 a man was executed for cutting down a tree, and cock fighting was still a popular sport in England.

In *War and Sport*, Pester describes an occasion when a party of four set out at four in the morning to deal with a tigress who had eluded them the day before, though they had picked up her cubs. The instant she heard them 'she came on most desperately, determined to rout them or die herself in the trial'. At a distance of thirty yards they gave her the contents of eight barrels, each loaded with two balls. She tumbled over, but in a moment

> 'recovered her legs and closed with the elephant nearest her, which she tore almost to pieces about the face, trunk and the breasts . . . After a most furious fight (which drove us almost *mad* with the pleasure it afforded us) the elephant shook the monster off and struck it a violent blow with the trunk.'

The italics in this and the succeeding extracts are Pester's.

There was a quarter of an hour of confusion before the tigress was finally killed.

> 'Our elephants were bellowing, and shewed every inclination to join in the combat; they seemed almost as furious as the parties engaged; in short we were *all mad together*.'

Summing up the whole adventure he concludes that

> 'it was the *thing impossible* for a small party to be more happy and comfortable than we were. We had *noble sport*, beside which we were doing no small service to the poor wretches who, with their little property, so constantly fell victims to the merciless monsters we destroyed, and they, poor devils, were most grateful to us in return for the good we did them, calling themselves "our slaves".'

That evening they dined at seven and 'drank "Tiger Hunting", "Fox Hunting" and "Hog Hunting" with each three times three'.

Yet Pester was a compassionate officer, devoted to his Indian soldiers, as they were to him; outstandingly courageous in battle in days when fighting was at close quarters and the personal bravery and example of the commander counted for even more than it does today. He and his friends were men of action and they took their pleasures as they fought their battles, and the border line between the two was not always very clearly defined. A man might cross and recross it in the course of the day. On 11th January 1803 Pester's battalion was part of a force laying siege to a town he calls Sarssnee. The assault was made four days later and the place captured after heavy fighting. But . . .

> 'being off duty this morning, Wemyss and myself injudiciously rode a couple of miles in rear of our camp with the greyhounds—this frolic was attended with the imminent risk of our lives, as the enemy had constantly strong parties of horse patrolling in the neighbourhood of our camp.'

They had excellent sport and returned to camp with their horses completely knocked up, but after an early dinner he marched with his company to relieve another battalion in the trenches.

It is not the cruelty, judged by today's standards, that is remarkable about their exploits: it is the almost reckless disregard of personal safety. There is a story in the *Oriental Sporting Magazine* of a party of four who had located a panther in a patch of cover. Each time he tried to break one of them would ride and try to engage him with the spear. When it was the turn of one Poins, the panther caught the horse, 'who broke away with his rump well clawed and his rider with the loss of a top from his Europe top boot, taken as clean off as if a Savigny had been applied'. Poins then suggested that they should dismount and attack on foot, and when his companions did not agree 'he took a short sabre with which he is in the habit of hunting in the right hand, and a strong spear in the left'. He had eight beaters armed with spears and one with a sword. The panther charged Poins, knocked him over and shook him as 'a terrier shakes a rat'. One of the beaters with great coolness took off his turban, put it around the animal's neck and dragged him off. As he turned on the man Poins cut him across the loins. Then there was a final charge. 'Showing his former partiality for his first antagonist, Poins, who was not to be done this time but gave him a dreadful cut in the neck, when in the act of springing on him, which nearly severed his head from his body; and after a few staggers he breathed his last.'

When the Mahratta wars were over, about 1810, the countryside began to settle down, troops were collected in cantonments and game became scarce in the immediate vicinity of military stations, but elsewhere it was still plentiful, and there were no game laws. You might have to travel forty or fifty miles to find something to shoot but there was no difficulty about that; parties of two or three would go into camp for a fortnight or even longer. With some semblance of law and order prevailing, the government, the East India Company as it still was, turned its attention to exploring the resources of what was really virgin forest. It was the day of Sanderson among the elephants in Mysore, Forsyth and Sterndale in the Central Provinces, men seconded for duty for the purpose. Their books mark the first serious attempt to record the natural history of the country, the customs of the people and the habits of the animals they shot.

In *Seonee* Sterndale draws a picture of Fordham, his central character.

> 'Clad in a close-fitting suit of stout drill, dyed with the barks of the mango and babool trees to the true shikar colour; the shoulders protected by pieces of leather to bear the friction of the rifle; leather-lined pockets in front to hold a small powder flask, caps, and balls, sewed up in a greased cloth; a kookri or Gurkha knife and a short-bladed, straight, double-edged dagger attached to a broad belt of sambhur leather; leggings of the same material completed his attire.'

He was the right man to have at your side at an awkward moment. He was out one evening with a young man who was in camp with him to learn something of the ways of the jungle. They rounded a corner in a forest path and met a tiger regarding them in a far from friendly way at a distance of three yards.

> '"Steady, my boy," he muttered between his teeth, "steady, my boy. Flinch not a muscle."'

The tiger turned round and disappeared into the jungle, and Fordham explained that given the least sign of uncertainty he would inevitably have attacked them.

Equally significant was the interest these men took in the customs and superstitions of the aboriginal tribes whose way of life in many cases had remained unaffected by any earlier invader of India. They grew to love them, to master their dialects, and to appreciate that they were indispensable allies for any man who set out to pit his wits against tiger or panther, buffalo or bison.

There was a freemasonry among sportsmen, a need for confidence on both sides. If you did not know what you were about you could hardly expect to be well served by a shikari. If you were experienced you knew instinctively when a good man appeared. Sanderson describes how after a time of disappointment a man came into his camp with news of buffalo:

> 'I saw at once he was the right person at last. There was no mistaking him. His appearance might not have been very prepossessing. He had a rough matted head of hair, and a string and a rag round his loins. But he was quiet and composed in his manner, and his replies confirmed the confidence I felt in him. I at once ordered out five elephants and gave my guide some tobacco. I recognised him as a brother come in the moment of my need.'

Forsyth describes a village shikari in the Central Provinces:

> 'A long gaunt figure clad in a ragged shirt of Mhowa green, with a dingy turban twisted round his shaggy locks, and furnished with the usual small-bored matchlock, with its bulky powder flask of bison's horn, and a smaller supply of priming powder kept carefully in the horn of a gazelle. His hearty services must be secured, however, for he alone knows intimately the ways and haunts of the tiger, and he alone will have the pluck to accompany you to mark him down.'

It is a curious fact that the lower down the scale of civilisation you move the more shackling is the hold of the supernatural on the simple minded; and when you were dealing with a man-eater the assistance of the local medicine man was essential. His it was to hold converse with the world of spirits, to cast omens, to compel the rain, to charm away the tiger or disease. And he looked the part.

> 'He is tall, thin and cadaverous, abstraction and mystery residing in his hollow eyes. When wanted, he has to be sent for to some distant haunt of gnomes and spirits, and comes with charms and simples slung in the hollow of a bottle-gourd. A

great necklace, fashioned with much carving from the kernels of forest fruits, marks his holy calling.'

You could not afford to scoff at local superstition; you did so at the risk of forefeiting the confidence of those who believed in it implicitly. You might even come across some manifestation of it for which you could find no rational explanation. In his book *Forest Life and Sport in India,* Eardley Wilmot tells the story of a party who had been trying without success to shoot a tiger. They were advised to consult the local wizard, a self-appointed official who was paid by the villagers to protect their cattle by his charms. For a fee of a kid and a bottle of rum he agreed that he could spare a tiger or two from his stock-in-trade. After some preliminary mumbo-jumbo he mounted an elephant and, murmuring incantations and ringing a small bell, he led the way to a miserable patch of grass that might at most have held a brace of partridge. But there was a tiger there, which walked majestically away for a few paces, then stood and offered an easy shot. They tried another patch of grass and another tiger came out and was duly shot. The wizard then decided that his stock was running low and left them to their own devices.

After a couple of blank days one of the party suggested that they might try to copy his methods. An oil lamp was lit and grains of rice and spices arranged in what seemed to be the same cabalistic pattern. They then mounted their elephants and, ringing the bell, went into the jungle. But they must have left out the magic word. A tiger appeared and, as though in a daze, walked across their front. Three shots fired at point-blank range missed him completely. Bewitched he may have been, he was not there to be shot.

# 3. Nimrods in Action

*Nimrod in action*

Since it was possible for Pester and his friends to give a charging tigress the contents of eight barrels, each loaded with two balls, without stopping her from severely mauling the nearest elephant, it is clear that compared with the rifles of today the weapons in use 150 years ago were not very much more than one jump ahead of the bow and arrow. It is true that they were flintlocks, not matchlocks, but they were muzzle loaders and a rifle heavy enough for dangerous game weighed twice as much as a modern 12-bore shotgun. The black powder they used enveloped the firer in a dense white cloud which hung round in the humid air of the jungle and obscured the view. Writing as late as the 1860s Kinloch reviews the newfangled breech loader and concludes that it was not so unreliable as it was made out to be; in fact no more so than the muzzle loader.

The effect of a bullet depends on its hitting power, which is the product of the muzzle velocity × the weight; but it is not quite so simple as that. You can kill as surely with a rapier as a lance, but the latter is more effective in halting a Whirling Dervish because of the greater shock imparted. Against dangerous game it was essential to use a heavy bullet, which if it did not kill outright would cripple and stop a charge.

The muzzle loader had the advantage that the weight of both bullet and charge of powder could be varied to suit individual taste, and there used to be 'great discussions round mess table and camp fire' as to what the best combination was. Even in those days there were some who advocated a comparatively light bullet with a high velocity, but Baker concludes that for stopping power there was nothing to touch a two- or three-ounce ball with eight to ten drams of good English powder behind it.

Sporting Rifles: Weights and Performance

| Weapon | Weight of black powder drams: or cordite grains† | Weight of bullet grains | Muzzle velocity ft/sec | Muzzle energy ft/lb | Energy at 100 yds ft/lb | Weight double-barrelled-rifle lb |
|---|---|---|---|---|---|---|
| 8-bore* 0·835″ | 10 dr BP | 1257 2·7 oz | 1500 | 6290 | 4010 | 16–18 |
| 12-bore* 0·729″ | 7 dr BP | 750 1·7 oz | 1550 | 4000 | 2420 | 11–12 |
| 0·577″ Express | 6 dr BP | 650 1·5 oz | 1650 | 3930 | 2730 | 11–12 |
| 0·475″ High velocity | 75 gr cordite 2·7 dr | 480 1·00 oz | 2175 | 5010 | 3860 | 11–12 |
| 0·375″ magnum | 60 gr cordite 2 dr | 300 0·5 oz | 2820 | 4150 | 3360 | 9½ |
| 0·275″ magnum | 44 gr cordite 1·5 dr | 180 0·3 oz | 2950 | 2770 | 2370 | 9½ |
| 12-bore magnum Paradox | A shotgun with the barrel rifled for the last few inches. Very effective up to 75 yds. | | | | | 8 |

* Generally muzzle loaders. † 27·3 grains = 1 dram = $\frac{1}{16}$ ounce.
The figures are taken from *Notes on Sporting Rifles*, by Major H. G. Burrard.

Improvements in sporting weapons followed on the heels of changes in the design and performance of military rifles; the most significant were the introduction of the magazine rifle and of cordite —smokeless powder—and the manufacture of steel strong enough to stand the pressure it set up in the breech. The table on the previous page shows details of two muzzle loaders, the ·577 express, which was the first breech loader, and three modern rifles. In the right-hand column is a figure which has not so far been considered: the weight of the rifle. In terms of physical effort there may not be much difference between carrying a rifle in the moist heat of the jungle or in the rarified air at a height of 18,000 feet; but in the hills you carried field-glasses and took your rifle only at the last moment, in the jungle you carried it yourself, always, or it might not be there when you wanted it. Eleven pounds is probably the limit which can be carried for long periods without distress.

To sum up, in the old days the 8-bore was the weapon for thick-skinned dangerous game; today, while the ·375 magnum is a remarkable all-round weapon, the ·475 H.V. gives a greater margin of safety against buffalo or tiger.

A popular vote would probably rate the tiger as providing the finest sport of all the Indian game animals. The more knowledgeable would qualify this by adding that much depends on how you set about it. Sanderson, on the other hand, awards the palm without hesitation to elephant shooting.

> 'It is difficult to define the exact elements which make elephant shooting the supremely exciting sport it is; but its danger and the necessity for the exercise of the sportsman's personal qualities of perseverance, endurance and nerve, are prominent ones. The best trackers can only bring their master up to the game, when everything depends on himself. The size of the noble beast; the fine line of country through which the chase always leads; and the fair stand-up nature of the encounter when the game is met—all tend to elevate elephant shooting above all sports with the rifle.'

Elephant shooting in India was never practised on anything like the same scale as was general in Africa. His home is in thick jungle among the foothills and in the early trigger-happy days the sportsman did not penetrate into these more remote areas. The comparative ease with which he could be caught and tamed, and his use for ceremonial occasions, for sport, forestry and heavy construction work, led to restrictions being placed on elephant shooting many years before it was thought necessary to pass game laws for the protection of other game animals. He was more valuable alive than dead.

In areas where the numbers were not kept down by capture, elephants could become a menace to cultivation, and even when restrictions were in force they might be lifted to deal with the occasional rogue which was threatening the lives of the villagers in jungle tracts. On the authority of 'the greatest of ancient or modern Nimrods', Sir Samuel Baker, elephant shooting ranks as the most dangerous of all sports if fairly followed for a length of time.

> 'The wild elephant's attack is one of the noblest sights of the chase. The cocked ears and broad forehead present an immense frontage; the head is held high, with the trunk curled between the tusks to be uncoiled at the moment of attack; the massive forelegs come down with the force and regularity of ponderous machinery; the whole figure is rapidly foreshortened, and appears to double in size with each advancing stride.'

An elephant may admittedly be shot without the sportsman being in any great peril; by coolness and good shooting it is possible to settle the matter with a single shot, but if he does charge the moment is one of supreme danger. The crux of the matter is that although it is as easy to hit an elephant as a haystack, the vital target is very small. The weight of bone, tissue and muscle virtually rule out the shot at the shoulder, and there remains only the brain, which even in a large animal measures no more than twelve inches by six. Located between the eye and the ear, it presents a constant target from the flank, but from the front allowance must be made for the rapidly changing angle of head and trunk; and in the heat of the moment it is by no means easy to pick the spot at which to fire.

Sanderson tells the story of his first attempt to shoot a rogue which had taken possession of eight miles of the road leading down from Mysore to the coast. When at length it killed two men on successive days it was decided that it must be shot. Trackers had located the animal the previous evening and he set out an hour before dawn the next day. After four hours they found him, but he was by then in such thick jungle that it was impossible to approach. They sat down to wait for six hours in a downpour of rain so heavy that it drowned the noise of the animal when it fed past them at close range. When the rain stopped they dried themselves and the rifles as best they could and took up the trail. After a mile they came up with the rogue. By crawling forward Sanderson got to within thirty yards, and was offered a shot which, though far from favourable, he decided to take as evening was drawing in. The effect was startling. The beast charged through the heavy curtain of smoke, which in the damp air hung like a fog, and passed within a yard of them. But it was no more than the instinctive reaction at being fired at. They followed a thick blood trail which showed that the bullet had passed through the skull, but it did not continue far and as night fell they had to give up the chase.

> 'I think I never in my life felt so disappointed. I had left Mysore in the hope of speedily returning in the proud role of successful rogue slayer. Myself and my men had been drenched to the skin and starved all day. To add to our discomfiture we were miles from home, to reach which our powers of walking and wading would be severely tried. Life had suddenly become a blank! I should never smile again!'

However, after a bath and a good meal, a hot toddy and a long cheroot, he felt better and two months later had the satisfaction of shooting the rogue. He found that from an imperfect knowledge of the structure of the skull he had at the first attempt aimed too high, and his shot had passed above the brain.

Even as long ago as the middle of the nineteenth century the rhinoceros had become very much less plentiful than most other varieties of big game. Fifty years later, his numbers still further reduced, he was to be found only in the Nepal Terai and the southern tip of Burma, and outside the ranks of the privileged few there can be hardly anyone alive today who has shot one.

In the Middle Ages there was a demand for his skin for the manufacture of shields, but when shields went out of fashion the only really marketable portion of his body was the horn. Ground to powder it fetched a high price as an aphrodisiac, particularly from the Chinese, and on this account there were always poachers ready to face the risks of going after him.

It is doubtful if the rhinoceros uses his horn to attack his enemies; nature provided it for the more utilitarian purpose of grubbing up roots and stripping the bark off trees. What is certain is that his most deadly weapons are his powerful incisor teeth, which he uses as a boar uses its tusks. There is a picture in *Oriental Field Sports* of a rhinoceros standing over an elephant lying on its side, bloodily disembowelled.

> 'In regions untrod by the foot of man he roams without fear or dispute as a monarch, to whom even the mighty elephant must give way, and before whose ponderous strength and weight the morose bull buffalo must bend the knee and kiss the dust.'

Even if the numbers had not dwindled to the point of scarcity it is doubtful if rhinoceros shooting would have made much appeal to the sportsman of more recent times. The attractions are the comparative rarity, the beauty of the dense wild surroundings in which he lived and the vast bulk and power of the beast. It would have been another matter if he could have been followed up and shot on foot, but the nature of the jungle he lived in ruled that out as a possibility. Writing a hundred years ago when sportsmen were less particular about what they shot, Baker concludes that there was not really very much to be said for it.

> 'Followed soon after dawn with two or three elephants, and patiently tracked up into its fastnesses till found and slain, it no doubt affords sport; but if put up surrounded by a great line of elephants and ultimately riddled with bullets and mobbed to death, it does not and cannot show much sport.'

If one accepts that the essential ingredients of any sport are skill, endurance and an element of danger, one can but agree with him.

He gives an account of a day when his party of four set out soon after daybreak with a line of eighteen elephants to beat through fields of young grass four or five feet high. Two rhinoceros were sighted at his end of the line. One bolted, the other halted about eighty yards from him, undecided what to do and half inclined to fight it out. As the animal turned and made off 'I let drive a two-and-a-half ounce steel-tipped conical at him' and a hundred yards away he fell stone dead, the bullet having raked him fore and aft. They killed two others that day and one the next. They were disappointed not to get a tiger as they were in country where they were generally plentiful, but 'enjoyed a good day's sport and made a large bag, both in weight and numbers, viz. a rhinoceros, five buffaloes, nine marsh and seven hog-deer, two peacocks, a floriken, five brace of "Kyah" partridge and a pink-headed duck'.

The early writers had little to say about the bison. He shared with the elephant a preference for remote and heavily wooded foothills where the only method of shooting was the slow and gruelling pursuit on foot with the help of trackers. They had not learnt to appreciate the attraction of this form of sport.

It was a very different story with the buffalo, who roamed in herds to be numbered in hundreds over the swampy plains of Bengal. More, perhaps, than any other animal he was the victim of reckless over-shooting. He was a curious mixture: confronted by a barrage of noise, a babel of human voices supported by a fusilade of shots, a herd would turn tail and bolt, but a bull who stood his ground was a formidable opponent.

> 'As brave as a boar, and as ferocious as a tiger or panther, a buffalo will often disdain to quit his ground, preferring rather to fight to the death, if unable to vanquish his assailant.
>
> 'Beside a remarkable ferocity, the buffalo displays a mean craftiness, unworthy of his vast size and strength, in concealing himself in the first piece of heavy jungle he comes to in his flight, and from its shelter suddenly charging upon his pursuers. Men and elephants have been frequently injured by such unexpected onslaughts, stalkers driven up into trees, and horsemen pursued out of the jungle, over the open, to a considerable distance.'

In the early days a select few might go in for stalking on foot, but more popular was shooting from a line of elephants, and these were the occasions when they were shot regardless of size or sex. Forsyth expresses the opinion that the prime sport is to go after the buffalo on horseback, though he adds that in the broken country of the Central Provinces it was difficult to find them on ground that could be ridden over. Baker, who shot in Bengal, also favoured riding, but there the going was easier.

> 'Riding down buffaloes on horseback on fairly good ground is excellent sport, and when the ground is indifferent or positively bad, the sport is exciting and even dangerous, demanding the utmost skill and care to avoid great peril to horse and rider.'

He describes an encounter when he was out with a friend, both 'mounted on fine Arabs, fleet and experienced hunters, bold as lions and sure-footed as goats'. They carried light double-barrelled rifles, handy for use on horseback. Villagers had come in begging them to shoot a bull which had turned vicious and killed two men. When they had located him they advanced, riding twenty yards apart, until they were within a hundred yards of where he stood, tossing his horns threateningly. He suddenly charged, and the hunt was up. The man attacked galloped away while the other ranged alongside and fired at the shoulder. The roles were then reversed. 'The game continued for as lively a half hour as ever I spent', and it was not until a dozen shots had been fired at point-blank range that he finally 'expired with a prolonged bellow of rage and pain'.

Riding a buffalo with the spear alone was out of the question

*Vicious Cow*

because of the weight of skin, bone and muscle, but there is an account in the *Oriental Sporting Magazine* of a hunt in which it was used as an auxiliary weapon to the rifle. The writers of those days were great versifiers. Their lyrics find no place in *The Oxford Book of English Verse*, they were meant to be sung in rousing chorus at the end of the day to a toast of three times three, but they bring vividly to life the spirit of the age. Their favourite topic was The Old Grey Boar, but occasionally they were inspired to write of other things, and here is an extract from *The Buffalo Hunt.* A party of horsemen armed with a miscellany of spears and rifles comes across a herd.

The noble monarch at their head
Paws up the ground with furious tread
 And lashes with his tail.
They yet irresolute appear
Till suddenly, as struck with fear,
Tossing their heads around they bear
 And thunder down the vale.

The chase is taken up.

Hunters rose and hunters fell
 In pressing o'er the crags,
But all of those who kissed the ground
And rising felt their bones were sound
Despising every minor wound
 Remounted quick their nags.

The chase was long but yet the strength
Of these great monsters failed at length
  And one was turned to bay;
Under a spreading pipal's shade
His stand for life he boldly made
His fierceness unallayed.
  By sunbeam's burning ray.
But nearly now and deadly hot
Were poured the lances and the shot,
  And gashed with many a wound
The noble beast to madness stung
Forth on his foes a moment sprung,
With one loud roar the jungles rung
  He sank upon the ground.

Elephant and buffalo might have their champions, but when all was said and done there was something distinctive about shooting a tiger; something the griffin, the young man freshly out from England, could quite literally write home about. Forsyth expresses the feeling:

> 'Many a man killed his forty or fifty tigers who has never succeeded in bagging, by fair stalking, a single bull bison or stag sambhar, yet there is a stirring of the blood in attacking an animal before whom every other beast of the jungle quails, and an unarmed man is helpless as the mouse under the paw of the cat—a creature at the same time matchless in beauty of form and colour, and in terrible power of offensive armature—something that draws men to its continued pursuit after that of every other animal has ceased to afford sufficient excitement to undergo the toil of hunting in a tropical country.'

Apart from all that, there was a practical aspect to it. In the very early days in Bengal tigers were so numerous as to be a real threat to the community. They might be seen in twos and threes along the public highway, and every year they were responsible for the deaths of hundreds of villagers. In 1782 Paul, a noted German shikari who lived in Calcutta, shot twenty-three in a week. They were comparatively plentiful till a much later date, and in the 1850s a district officer in the Central Provinces, who should have known better, shot sixty in two years before handing over his district on promotion.

The elephant as an animal you shot from, not at, is the key figure in nearly all the tiger-shooting stories of the early days. The sportsman on the back of an elephant was faced with a problem familiar enough to gunnery officers of the Royal Navy and tank crews of the Royal Armoured Corps: how to shoot from a moving platform. It was, moreover, a platform that apart from the eccentricities of pitch and roll might without warning change direction by 180°.

To be able to take a snap shot from the back of a moving beast was the outcome of much practice, but it was something the sportsman had to learn to do. He could hardly expect to win the confidence of the mahout unless he could demonstrate his ability to shoot fast, shoot straight and keep on shooting in an emergency.

A good elephant was the sportsman's best friend, and simplified tasks that would otherwise have been difficult or extremely dangerous. A bad elephant was a danger to life and limb. If he took fright and bolted those on his back ran the risk of being swept off by overhanging branches. In the words of one who had experience in the matter: 'You might as well try to halt a bolting elephant as stop a railway engine by hooking a walking stick round the funnel.' There is a story of an elephant which was slightly mauled before the tiger that attacked it was shot dead at its feet. It disgraced itself by bolting, the howdah and its occupants being swept off as it passed under a low overhanging branch. That evening the elephant was rubbed down with the fat of the tiger and its staunchness was never again in question.

The elephant could not travel over broken, trappy country but was invaluable in high grass or thick undergrowth. It was reckoned that the best sport was had with a line of ten, three or four carrying the guns, with pad elephants in between. With a larger number, control and discipline became difficult. It was usual to have rifles posted as stops to deal with anything that did not wait for the line to reach it, but for any Nimrod worth his salt a post as one of the stops was considered a very poor form of sport. They preferred to be in the thick of it, rockets firing, tom-toms beating, with the chance of a shot at point-blank range to quicken the blood. To sit in a machan was held to be taking an unfair advantage of the tiger, and sitting up over a kill was rated as the last resort of the idle and unenterprising.

Forsyth's view was that the finest way of tiger shooting, the *crême de la crême* of the sport, was for a man to shoot on his own, in the fierce hot months before the monsoon when cover was less dense, setting out after breakfast on a single elephant, in search of a known tiger over a well reconnoitred piece of ground. Both elephant and mahout had to be trained for this sort of work. If they were, then the elephant was very much more than just a mount to carry you through the jungle. He would take an active and intelligent interest in the proceedings, and could almost learn to talk. His vocabulary was limited, consisting of a single word, but it could never be misunderstood. An elephant on the scent strikes the end of his trunk on the ground, producing a sound like the tap of a drum. He never makes this sound except when he is close on a tiger. A writer in the *Oriental Sporting Magazine* describes a famous animal named Hyder Guj.

> 'He was one of the best in India. I have seen him discover a tiger with as much ease as a pointer would a partridge. He makes the sound above described and points with his trunk in the direction in which the tiger is lying; the mahout has no occasion to guide him for he will carry you straight up to the tiger's lair or tear away the bushes which conceal him. When the tiger is discovered, Hyder stands as steady as a rock until you have fired, and if the tiger is only wounded will follow with apparently as much eagerness as the sportsman in the howdah; if killed, will put up his trunk for his well-earned *seer* of *gur* (two pounds of rough brown sugar).'

Considering again the comparative stopping power of the rifles in use in those days it is not surprising to find a number of stories where things went wrong and a tiger managed to establish a foothold on the elephant before it was killed. Fatal accidents were more common than in recent times, and on the opposite page is an extract from some notes on tiger shooting written about 1843, which gives the names of five officers known to the writer who lost their lives while so engaged.

If you were unlucky enough to be mauled by a tiger the treatment you received was somewhat below modern standards. The author of *The Royal Bengal Tiger* was an officer in the Indian Medical Service and describes a case that came to his notice.

> 'An officer who had wounded a tiger followed it on foot and came on it in high grass; he fired as it charged and mortally wounded the brute which however had the strength to seize him by the shoulder, inflicting severe wounds. The tiger actually fell over dead, his jaws closed on the officer's shoulder. The wounds were washed and ligatured in the jungle, prior to removal to Roorkee. On examination the shoulder was found greatly swollen, the ligatures so tense as to necessitate their division. There were two extensive lacerated wounds on the front of the deltoid and two corresponding to them on the back. The spine

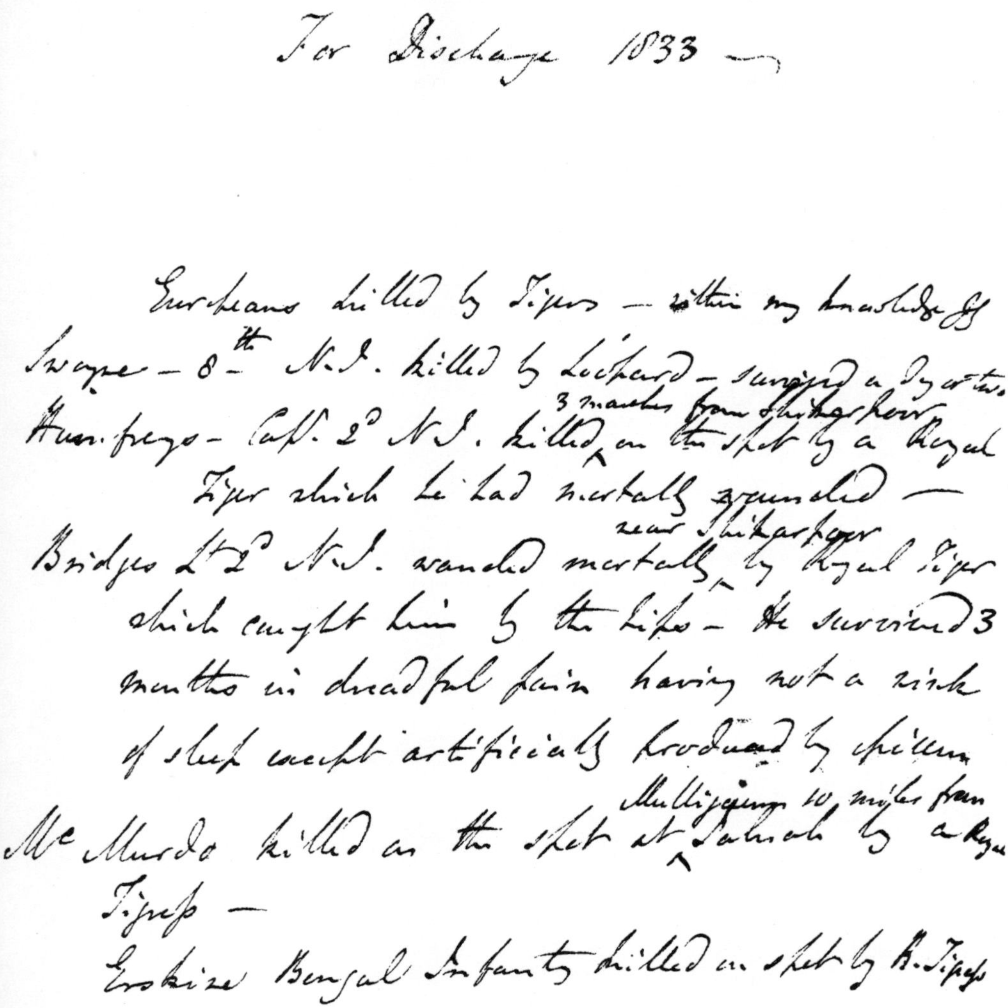


*From an old Diary*

of the scapula was fractured about its centre. The nervous shock which followed the accident was excessive and for about fifteen days the patient's mind was quite unsettled, his ideas wandering and disconnected, his eyes staring, tongue coated, pulse varying from 133, or fluttering with intermissions. Any attempt at fixing the limb aggravated the symptoms and the idea was abandoned. The sloughing and discharge from the wounds was at first very great but improvement manifested itself in this as in all other respects from about the twentieth day. The limb continued powerless but general health and condition of mind daily

> improved. Treatment consisted in a thorough cleaning of the wounds with solution permanganate of potash, and their subsequent treatment with carbolic oil, bark and ammonia in effervescence, with generous diet prescribed daily. Those who fall into the tiger's clutches do not always escape so fortunately.'

They had strange ideas about diseases generally. It was universally accepted that malaria, or jungle fever, was contracted through breathing the unwholesome air that arose from damp ground. Various preventative measures were suggested. One man had a half circle of fires kept burning up wind of his camp so that the warm air wafted the poisonous vapours over his head. Another thought they could be dispelled by smoking cheroots.

The early Nimrods were the founders of a great tradition. Life in civil station or cantonment might be petty and boring, but there was no lack of excitement for those who chose to go in search of it. It could never be boring, it might be dangerous; it would seldom be easy, you won success in the sweat of your brow. And they were men with a tremendous zest for the good things of life. When the hero of *Seonee* got back to breakfast after a start before dawn he expected to find ready for his repast 'omelettes and kitchree, dry curries, a round of cold corned beef, potted wild duck, eggs, toast and chupattis'. At the end of the day he and his young friend gathered round a roaring fire after 'a hearty dinner of soup, sanwal fish from the lake, a roast haunch of black buck, pintail duck and blue bull marrow bones, with a bottle of good Burgundy'.

Forsyth was firmly of the opinion that although every sensible man in India spends his Christmas in the jungle he need not forgo the traditional fare.

> 'We spent a Christmas of considerable joviality in that remote wilderness, dinner consisting of a peacock and sambar tongue, supported by roast haunch of red deer venison, as *pièces de résistance*, with cheetal cutlets and fillets of nilgai veal as *entrées*, followed up by boiled quails and roasted teal, and concluded by the orthodox plum-pudding and mince pies out of tins. Sundry glasses of whiskey toddy, imbibed round a rattling bonfire in front of the tents, were fully justified by the really severe cold after sunset.'

No one went into the jungle without a good supply of claret, and it is by no means uncommon to read of an exceptional day's sport being celebrated by cracking a couple of bottles of well-iced champagne.

And they were full of ideas as to how to display their trophies to the best advantage.

> 'Elephant's feet make unique footstools. The nails should be scraped till quite white, and the skin covered with a coating of lamp black. Both skin and nails should then be varnished, and the top of the foot covered with panther's skin, secured round the edge by large-headed silver nails, and a velvet band. Small feet make good cheroot boxes for the table with a mahogany tray inside, partitioned off for different sizes, and a mahogany or silver lid, surmounted by a small silver elephant to lift it off by. They can also be made up into tobacco boxes, ink stands, or small boxes for a lady's table.'

One can picture the Old Shikari bashfully placing one in the hands of 'her he loved'.

# THE SPEAR

# 4. Early Days

*About to throw*

The sport of hoghunting, or pigsticking as it was later called, consists of the finding and pursuit of the wild boar by mounted sportsmen armed with a spear. After being chased, often for a mile or more, the boar becomes tired and annoyed and charges the hunter and, after a short or long battle, is killed, usually by a spear driven through his heart. This bare statement quite fails to account for the spell it cast over those who took part in it. Foxhunting is said to be the King of Sports and the Sport of Kings, but anyone who has ever ridden after and killed a boar is certain that pigsticking is the finest sport of them all.

More than any other it inspired those who wrote the songs that were sung round the camp fire at the end of the day.

Over the valley, over the level,
Through the dak jungle ride like the devil
There's a nullah in front but a boar as well,
So damn the nullah and ride like hell.

About 1800, the planters of Behar used to hunt the sloth bear with dogs, out of the cane fields into the grass of the open country where he could be ridden and speared. After a few years the bears tired of this amusement and retired to the heavy forest where the ground was unrideable. The hunters then turned their attention to the wild boar. The idea spread to Calcutta, capital of the Bengal Presidency, and then to Bombay. Hunters originally rode singly or in pairs, but when the sport became popular, went out in groups of five or six and organised themselves as tent clubs. The one started at Poona claims to be the oldest in India, being founded at the time of the British occupation in the Peshwa's days before the battle of Kirkee in 1817.

The earliest records come from *Oriental Field Sports* where the plates show small parties in hard jockey caps, armed with long throwing spears, chasing boar which had been beaten out of high sugar-cane crops.

> 'The first who can get within proper distance throws his spear, aiming at the hog's head and filing off to make room for the next. I have seen a spear, thrown by a remarkably strong man at a hog moving at some yards distance in a parallel direction, dart through both shoulder blades, passing all but eight inches of shaft out at the opposite side. If the hog be very much exhausted, a person with a strong hand may await the charge and stab the spear between the shoulder blades and ribs or strike the forehead, by either of which methods the hog's course may be usually stopt.'

These spears, thrown like javelins, were some ten feet long and had heavy triangular heads. Williamson offers this advice.

> 'The best distance for delivering a spear is when the horse is about six feet behind the hog and nearly as much to the left, then turn your horse to the left immediately after delivering the spear, avoiding the charge and preventing him from ripping your horse. If it misses the hog and the point does not stick into the ground, the rider must dismount and pick it up, and by the time he has remounted hogs have often escaped.'

In 1830 another method of spearing, invented by Mr Mills, became general; the spear was shortened to about six feet six inches, the shaft of stout, solid male bamboo with a lighter diamond-shaped head, balanced by a lead weight on the butt. This spear was grasped near the butt end and used overhand, driven down at close quarters into the hog. This 'short' spear was used until 1938 by the Calcutta Tent Club as being most effective in the thick jungles in which they hunted. It was found that the hog when closely pressed usually turned and charged the hunter, enabling him to drive the spear well home, balking the hog's attack and allowing the rider to get clear while still keeping a hold of his weapon. When used skilfully this method was deadly, as the spear often penetrated the hog's heart or backbone and he died at once. But with a less bold pig who jinked—twisted and turned in his gallop—the short spear was less effective and soon another method came to be generally adopted.

*Return from Hunting*

This was the 'long' spear, used underhand, eight to nine feet long, still with a narrow steel head and weighted at the butt. This method was adopted all over India except in the Calcutta Tent Club who to the end never favoured it. It had the advantage of about two feet of reach both when spearing and when holding off the pig. Moreover, when overtaking a pig which was reluctant to charge the rider could effectively spear him as he galloped alongside.

The *Oriental Sporting Magazine* frequently carried reports of the activities of the various tent clubs. In 1828 at Deesa, two hundred miles north of Bombay, six men killed 22 hog on a ten day trip. In 1831 five on a trip near Poona killed 34 in six days. The 'Nuggur Hunt' at Ahmednagar was a very active body. A party of seven in seventeen days killed 110. A breakdown of this figure shows that only 25 of these were what would today be considered warrantable pig; boar standing at least 28 inches at the shoulder. One boar had a two-inch piece of broken off tush embedded in its face, the result of a battle with another boar which, by a coincidence, was killed the following day with a broken tush exactly fitting the missing piece. Of the bag, 50 were squeakers and 35 were sows. The killing of sows was then common, but later became forbidden, the Calcutta Tent Club in 1862 making a fine of one dozen of champagne on anyone who killed one. Elsewhere the fine was usually 'one gold mohur'—fifteen rupees. Not that the sow was any less formidable than the boar.

> 'When boars are scarce, the sportsmen are glad to pursue fat sow, these run faster than a boar and their bite is very severe. I was hunting near Lye with a gentleman who, on overtaking a sow, jabbed his spear into her, the horse reared and the sow laid hold of the gentleman's toe with her teeth, to which she held fast pulling with all her strength. In a few minutes the top of his boot came away with part of his toenail, the agony of which produced faintness. Luckily the sow cleared off with the spear in her back and I was able to assist my friend. Severe falls frequently occur and it is desirable to carry a lancet. I have saved many lives after such falls by being able to draw off blood immediately on the spot. A wounded boar is a very formidable animal and it is better to let him escape than to run the risk of being made a cripple.'

The spear has claimed other victims. In *Cavalry Surgeon* there is a story of a clash with a party of mounted enemy at the time of the Mutiny.

> 'Fortunately the adjutant of Beatson's Horse of the Irregular Cavalry, Clay, a bold and intrepid pigsticker was to the front and we dashed on them in some sort of line. They drew up in close order to receive our charge but, not liking the pace, broke and fled. Our men followed right well and the adjutant and myself set to work in earnest with our hog spears, made by Bodraj of Aurangabad. Clay was shot through the helmet and spear handle but otherwise unhurt. One of our best men lost his bridle arm which was completely severed by a sabre cut but, twisting a piece of turban round it, he begged me that I would not let it trouble me until we reached camp.'

A quarry only slightly less dangerous than man was the tiger. In 1803, Sir Robert Gillespie on hearing that a tiger had escaped from a menagerie, borrowed a lance from a Native Cavalry Officer and despatched it on Bangalore racecourse. One may be sure that Pester would have a story about some such exploit.

> 'Major Robert Nairn of the Bengal Native Cavalry was a great favourite of the Commander-in-Chief, General Lake, who once saw him spear a tiger on horseback, the only man probably to attempt so rash and desperate a thing.'

General Lake intervened and shot the tiger and sent the skin and the broken spear home to the Prince of Wales.

Another formidable character was General James Outram who seems to have made a habit of tackling tigers with the spear.

> 'In 1828 having heard of some tigers Outram sharpened his old Maratha lance which had a knob of rusty iron on one end and a bayonet like a bit of steel on the other and set out. The tiger got into a hole and we smoked it out. Outram stood above the hole and speared him in the neck as he came out. The tiger turned and broke the spear in pieces, when Tapp and I (Douglas Graham, Outram's adjutant) fired and knocked him over.'

And there is a story of one Adam Durnford Gordon, who, armed only with a common hog spear and a sharp sabre and mounted on an Arab, used to kill tigers single handed on open ground. Regrettably there are no details of how he did it.

A beat for pig might disturb a panther. Only a brave man on a very bold horse would tackle him and it was taken for granted that whoever first speared a panther had to finish off the animal himself.

> 'Spearing leopard is a nasty business. I have on occasion speared three leopards myself. On the north bank of the Sarda river in Oudh a very large leopard jumped out of a grass clump, snarled and ran off. I was on a very fast horse but did not catch him for about 3,000 yards, when he squatted. My spear went through him deep into the ground and he rolled over as I speared. They do this. Lionel Hearsey of the Royal Dragoons kindly gave me his spear with which I broke the leopard's spine at the next attempt. When I thanked him for giving me his spear he said, "I thought you had wounded him the first time." This is quite right and proper as a wounded leopard is a very nasty customer. Hearsey had a wounded leopard on his horse behind the saddle a couple of days before this.'

Wolf, nilghai and hog deer were often hunted with the spear but there is only one story of anyone tackling a crocodile. He was one 'Empty Sahib', an Indian corruption of the name Armitage.

> 'Captain Darrock of the Argyles was riding with "Empty" when the latter spotted an eight or ten foot mugger crocodile in a shallow pool cut off from the main river. "Empty" said that anyone could kill a mugger with a spear, so he slipped off his horse and went for the mugger and the mugger for him. His tactics were very sound and consisted of getting to the mugger's near foreleg and staying there. "There," said "Empty", "the mugger cannot bite you or break your leg with a stroke of his tail." The mugger got hold of the first two spears with his teeth and made matchwood of them. "Empty" successfully disengaged both times, dragged Darrock's best spear out of his hand and finished the mugger off with it, the spear being chewed to pieces before the beast died.'

But now to our main adversary, the boar.

# 5. The Tent Clubs

*On-on-on*

Besides the hoghunter there were three other parties to the sport of pigsticking: the boar, the horse and the beater. 'Pig', as he is called by those who hunt him, can grow to a very large size, one is recorded in 1855 as measuring 44 inches at the shoulder and weighing over 400 lb, 25 stone of fighting fury. But most pig hunted measured between 28–34 inches, weighing between 120–260 lb. Pig under that limit were not hunted and anyone rash enough to spear one was fined a golden mohur for the benefit of tent club funds.

The boar is a combination of speed, cunning and ferocity who fights to the end with the utmost courage. He has a short back tapering to lower hind legs, a solid mass of hard muscle, attacking with bristles erect and grunting savagely, and it takes a bold man and horse to face him when his blood is up. At his business end he keeps a pair of sharp curved tushes up to nine inches long, which can rip up man and horse. Even the tiger avoids him and may pay the penalty if he takes him on. For his tough make and shape he is surprisingly fast and can outpace a thoroughbred at full gallop over half a mile, and he is so handy that at full stretch he can turn through a right angle to jink and throw off his hunter. After that he soon tires and then relies on his cunning and ferocity. If lucky, a single spear thrust may kill him, but more often he makes off and, though tired, charges the horseman again and again until killed by a final spear through the heart: fighting to the end, a very brave opponent.

The horse had to be able to remain upright when galloping full tilt through thick grass six to nine feet high, over ground as hard as rock, seamed with large and small nullahs and the occasional sunken buffalo wallow. It was amazing how a good horse managed to keep a spare leg in reserve when his leading foot touched nothing; 'nothing' being the bottom of a wallow as much as three feet deep. One well-known horse with only one eye, would turn at full gallop into high grass on his blind side, drop into a wallow and remain upright, possibly by second sight or sense of touch of his hoof.

Falls were fairly frequent over such country but seldom serious as at the speed at which the horse was galloping he and his rider would fall end over end without too much damage: a slow fall was much more dangerous. Old, disused wells, completely overgrown by long grass, were a constant hazard in the Meerut and Muttra countries, and in 1890 a Colonel Napier fell into one and broke his neck. The only other fatal accident fall on record was in 1934 when Lieut. Ferguson-Davie was killed instantaneously. He was a confident and experienced horseman and a very fine spear and was hunting a pig ahead of his heat on a young horse which fell and rolled over him.

A skilled rider, holding off the charging pig with his spear, relied on the impetus of his horse to carry him clear before his adversary could charge home. If he did not manage to do so a horse might be cut from heel to knee.

The horses used by the early hunters about 1800 were country bred, but about 1830 Arabs were being imported. They were bold, fast and handy. A colour print, published by Fores in 1836, shows the riders wearing top hats and white kid gloves, with luxuriant side whiskers, mounted on high class Arabs. Fourteen hands and under, they seem small by modern standards and as some of the pig they met measured up to 40 inches at the shoulder, the tushes must have reached nearly to the rider's knees: a nasty thought. Later 'Walers', horses bred in New South Wales, were imported but a writer in *The Oriental Sporting Magazine* in 1856 expressed the view that Walers would never hold their own with Arabs against pig. With improved breeding the country bred, often with considerable Arab strain, again came into their own.

The Kadir Cup was to pigsticking what the Grand National is to racing: a name familiar to sportsmen all over the world.

'Carclew', a country bred, won the cup three times in 1924–25–27 and 'Manifest', also a country bred, won three times. 'Carclew' had an unequalled record, competing in the semi-final or final in seven successive years from 1923–30. His owner, Captain Scott-Cockburn, then took him back to England where he died in 1932 at the great age of 32 years. His owner's description of him describes the ideal horse after pig.

> 'Carclew really loved a hunt. At the cry "*woh jata*" (there he goes) I could feel his heart thumping between my legs; once a boar had been singled out he would follow him as a greyhound will a hare. In the open he would place me right to spear within a

minute. In thick tamarisk or grass it was no more necessary for me to steer him than in the open. Whenever we lost a pig it was either in impenetrable thorn, or when the cover was over my head. I think he must have accounted for a good third of the 500 odd boar on which I got "first spear". In ten years' hunting he was never cut by a pig nor missed his turn.'

The rank and file of the beaters came from the villages adjoining the stretch of land hunted over. In the Meerut, Delhi and Muttra Tent Club country the best of them were Aherias or Kanjars, men of gypsy tribes, untouchable members of the lowest level of Hindu society. They were a cheerful race whose ostensible occupation was weaving grass into brushes or roofs for huts and bullock carts, but they were adept thieves, not very popular with their neighbours and in constant trouble with the police. Barefoot, clad only in a loincloth and pagri, and carrying a stout pole, a hundred of them in line would beat through the high grass until a rideable boar emerged with a savage 'woof-woof' from a thicket. And all for a few annas a day. There was, however, another attraction. Fox hunting has been described as the 'unspeakable in full pursuit of the uneatable', but pigsticking has the edge on it as pork was considered a great delicacy by the beaters, who could rarely if ever afford to eat meat.

In charge of them was the head shikari. Some of these men had remarkable records, one Chamru served the Muttra Club from before the Boer War until hunting ended in 1947. An article in the *Hog Hunters Annual* describes the bond that existed between these men and the tent clubs they served.

'When one considers that some Hon. Secs. have been young subalterns with but a brief experience of India, it speaks well of both parties that the loyalty and devotion which they receive from these shikaris has never been shaken. Something of this may be ascribed to the fact that among Hon. Secs, no less than among shikaris, a great tradition has been handed down.'

The writer goes on to speak of General Wardrop, the best known of modern pigstickers. 'No words of mine can better epitomise the ascendancy he had over these men than an expression one of them used to me: "To us", he said simply, "he is like God."'

In the same number of the Annual there is a short biographical sketch of Dhanni, Saugor Tent Club shikari from 1882–1927.

'To match his wits against those of the pig is the height of Dhanni's ambition. Money is a secondary consideration; it is sport that appeals to him. Two words, familiar to most of us, find no place in his vocabulary; the one is Fear, the other is Fatigue. He knows neither. Very familiar is the scene when a wily old boar has come off the end of a hill, lain up in a bush and been marked down. The line will be stopped and silenced as if by magic. Dhanni will advance, supported by a dozen or so of his trusted stalwarts and breathing foul oaths against the tribe of pig in general, and this boar in particular. How many of us, bare-legged and armed only with a lathi, would care to advance on a bush known to contain a large and angry boar? How many of us again could conduct a line from 7.30 a.m. till 5 p.m. in the hot weather over rocky hills and scrub jungle at the age of nearly eighty, with only a sip of water as refreshment? Yet Dhanni will not only do this, but after it all will start off, to all appearance as fresh as paint, to tramp the ten odd miles to his home!'

The success of pigsticking depends very much on good organisation, and from 1840, as British control over India extended, a number of tent clubs were founded for this purpose. Very early ones were at Delhi, Cawnpore and Meerut and the countryside, through which the rivers Jumna, Ganges and Gogra flowed and changed their course over the years, was thick with cover which held hundreds of pig. The places at which tent clubs are known to have been founded are shown on the map on pages 32 and 33.

To those who hunted pig it was a way of life: interludes of work necessary to earn their pay, with the weekend hunting to look forward to. Hunt club members would ride out in company to camp in mango groves and hunt on alternate weekends. About 1870, a benevolent commander-in-chief decreed that except for essential work Thursday would be observed as a holiday. Saturday and Sunday did not count as working days, and it was pointless to return to barracks for a single day's work on Friday, so a pigsticking week-end lasted from Wednesday till Sunday evening. Everyone was presumed to work extra hard from Monday to the Wednesday of the following week. The dedicated pigsticker saved to buy another or a better horse, to be trained to docility and obedience in the evenings: a pig-shy horse who refused to face a charging boar was a disaster to be passed on at the first opportunity. Much of the evening conversation was of meets and pig; incredibly boring to those who did not share his sport.

The success or failure of a tent club depended on the honorary secretary, responsible for all the work of organisation, and in the field, as complete a dictator as a master of foxhounds. The real business of the weekend began after dinner on the first evening when the honorary secretary arranged the heats, two or three spears hunting together; by lots if all were more or less experienced or, if there were unskilled riders out, arranging the heats so that there was at least one good spear in each.

Breakfast was at dawn or soon after and the spears rode out to where the beaters were extended waiting for them, with the head shikari on a pony or a camel, two or three yards between each man, and a large red flag on either flank.

The heats take station at equal distances along and behind the beaters and the line starts, in comparative silence lest they disturb a distant pig. Through the long grass go the beaters, tapping each thicket with their poles, for pig sit tight, and when disturbed come out like a rocket. When a pig is flushed the head shikari or the nearest flag bearer yells '*Woh jata*', and sets off in pursuit, waving his flag to show the nearest heat that a pig is away. The heat gallops up and taking up the line starts the hunt. The first thing they have to settle is whether the pig is 'rideable', sows and boars under 120 lbs being strictly preserved. After the first 100 yards the nearest spear will decide. If he is not rideable he signals to the others by holding his spear horizontally at arm's length. If all is well he gallops on, shouting 'on-on-on', and the hunt is up.

The leading rider gallops on the line of the pig, as close to him as he can get, with the other two spears fanned out on either side, so that if the pig jinks one of the others can take up the running. If the grass is sparse the pig's back will show above it but more usually it may be up to six feet high and his passage can be seen only by the waving of tops as he gallops through it. The boar will almost certainly be making for some safe haven, a thick impenetrable patch of tamarisk or thorn jungle. He will pick the roughest ground, cut by nullahs, which his instinct tells him is good for him and bad for his pursuers.

For the first half mile spears will not be able to come up with him owing to his great speed over this distance, but he then begins to tire and the leading spear comes up on his tail. He then begins to jink, the spear on the line loses sight of him and the one on the flank takes up the hunt, echoing the cry, 'on-on-on', the pleasantest sound in the world to the pigsticker's ear. As well as jinking he may suddenly squat motionless on the ground to throw off his pursuers.

When he realises that he will not make his haven his next object is to attack the hunter. As the leading spear gallops up alongside, the pig cocks his ears and with a vicious 'woof-woof' turns at full speed with the object of cutting his enemy with his tushes. As he comes in

*Kadir Cup*

the rider lowers his spear and at the last moment drives it home, aiming at the heart. If he is successful the pig dies at once, if not, the rider must hold him off for a split second as he swings his horse clear and disengages the spear. Even though wounded the pig may still be full of running and able to escape by jinking, but at last he sinks on his hind quarters and receives the *coup de grâce* through the heart. Ground, cover and the skill of the hunters vary considerably but even with the odds so loaded against him roughly two out of three pig that are hunted make good their escape.

The hunt is over and the rider who was the first to spear the pig can claim his tushes in the evening. By some miracle one of the flag men appears and ties a piece of rag to the nearest bush to mark the spot. In due course four men arrive, tie the dead boar to a stake and carry him back to camp to be measured, recorded in the log then handed over to provide a feast of pork for the beaters. The heat make their way back, change horses, sharpen their spears, take a drink of cold tea from the *char-wallah* (tea boy) and resume their stations behind the line. In a temperature that may be well over 100° in the shade it is no sport for the unfit, the indifferent rider or the half-hearted.

By midday everyone will have had enough; they return to camp and after a quick lunch with plenty of cold beer the spears retire to their tents to sleep away the afternoon. In the evening they visit the horse lines to see that all is well, then gather in the mess tent to discuss the day's sport while the honorary secretary writes up the log. A typical entry in the Delhi Tent Club log reads:

28th May 1926 Kasna (2nd Day)

| *Right heat* | *Centre Heat* | *Left heat* |
|---|---|---|
| Cursetjee (I.M.S.) | Templer R.A. (Hon Sec.) | West R.H.A. |
| Ruttledge (Poona Horse) | Chapman R.A. | Phipps R.H.A. |

Beat Kasna jhow (tamarisk) and bend of river, small pig lost by centre in jhow. Crossed river (Jumna), and beat thick grass. Right hunted a good boar till the doctor (Cursetjee), took a heavy toss, laid out for 10 minutes, lost two teeth. Many pig in Chaurpore Kadir. Left heat, after a fast hunt killed a small one. Centre picked up a scarred old warrior who fought well. Left hunted one a long way through nullahs, and eventually lost it in jhow. Later right hunted and killed a good boar, which broke back. Nice days hunting, very hot.

| | | | | |
|---|---|---|---|---|
| 213th boar | Phipps | 'Cis' | 27 inches | 120 lbs |
| 214th boar | Templer | 'Aaron' | 31 inches | 180 lbs |
| 215th boar | Ruttledge | 'Chinatown' | 29 inches | 152 lbs |

The second boar had fine tushes measuring 9 inches, a local record. Now reached the best bag since the war.

Another and very exciting way of hunting pig was by 'gooming'. Spears ride out a couple of hours before dawn to the edge of thick cover. Pig usually feed at night on the grass of the river bed and return to cover at dawn. As the light grows, the old pig followed by his wife and children are seen in the distance, and spears gallop towards him to come up with him before he can escape into the thick unrideable tamarisk on the river bank. The boar will try to escape by clever jinking, and he very often succeeds in doing so.

Away from the beds of the big rivers in north India the pig live on the low thorn-covered hills. The beaters work through the cover; the spears are stationed round the edge and try to cut the boar off as he makes for the next hill.

There were also plenty of pig to be found outside the territory of the organised tent clubs, and a couple of sportsmen on ten days leave at Christmas and hoping for a mixed bag would take their horses and their spears as well as rifle and shot gun.

As with most sports, pigsticking had its competitive side, the Kadir Cup (held by the Meerut Tent Club since 1871) being the best known event. This was a competition for first spear. Every rider could enter two horses and there would often be over fifty entries. Heats of three were drawn and when a pig got up, the umpire who accompanied it gave the order 'ride'. They galloped off each trying to spear the pig and draw first blood. The first to do so showed his spear to the umpire and went into the next round while the rest of the heat continued the hunt until the pig escaped or was killed. Experience and a very fast horse were necessary. The illustration on page seventy-two shows an incident in the competition for 1925. It carries the legend 'Marsh missing his pig and letting in Captain Scott-Cockburn, the eventual winner'.

If it was the dream of most pigstickers to win the Kadir Cup, it would also be their ambition to be a member of the winning team in the Muttra Cup, open to teams of three from any tent club or regiment. Each team rode six or eight heats and the prize went to the one that killed the most pig. It was a truly sporting event with no striving for first spear. The names of some of the winners of both competitions are shown on page 75.

The Kadir Cup was an annual award. The winner received the entry fees at Rs.15 a horse and with the money bought a replica of the cup. The trophy won in 1890 by Captain J. Hanwell R.A. stands proudly among the regimental silver in the Royal Artillery Mess at Woolwich. It would be a fitting home for the Muttra Cup also; there, or in the Cavalry Club, but fate has ruled otherwise. The silver boars have been removed from the plinth and the cup is awarded annually for the Light Weight Race of the Army Point to Point Association. Many will think it has been misappropriated.

## THE TENT CLUBS

There was one other small award, within the reach of many who perhaps never aspired to win the Kadir, the tent club button. As the tailpiece to this chapter is a facsimile of the button which was granted to members of the Meerut Tent Club who got ten first spears. And proud they were to wear it.

The first Bengal planter, turning his attention from bear to boar, can never have imagined that the sport of hoghunting which he

WINNERS OF THE KADIR AND MUTTRA CUPS

| Year | Kadir Cup | | Muttra Cup |
|---|---|---|---|
| 1883 | Lieut Baden-Powell | 13th Hussars | |
| 1908 | Lord Kensington | | |
| 1909 | Mr Vernon | 60th Rifles | |
| 1910 | Mr Paynter | R.H.A. | |
| 1911 | Mr Bromilow | 14th Lancers | |
| 1912 | Captain Gatacre | 11th Lancers | |
| 1913 | Mr Sherston | 11th Lancers | |
| 1914 | Captain Medlicott | Skinners Horse | |
| 1919 | Percy Marsh | I.C.S. | |
| 1920 | Captain West | R.H.A. | |
| 1921 | Captain Davison | 2nd Lancers | 7th Hussars |
| 1922 | Captain Baldwin | 11/12th Lancers | Lucknow Tent Club |
| 1923 | Mr Bates | R.F.A. | Meerut Tent Club |
| 1924 | Captain Scott-Cockburn | 4th Hussars | No competition* |
| 1925 | Captain Scott-Cockburn | ,, ,, | ,, ,, |
| 1926 | Captain Catto | ,, ,, | 4th Hussars |
| 1927 | Captain Scott-Cockburn | ,, ,, | Muttra Tent Club / R.A. Training Centre } Tie |
| 1928 | Captain Richards | R.A. | 4th Hussars B. |
| 1929 | Captain Head | 4th Hussars | No competition |
| 1930 | Captain Richards | R.A. | ,, ,, |
| 1931 | Captain Richards | R.A. | ,, ,, |
| 1932 | Mr Jones | 10th Hussars | ,, ,, |
| 1933 | Captain Grenfell | 9th Lancers | Meerut Tent Club |
| 1934 | Mr Gray | Skinners Horse | Muttra Tent Club / 10th Hussars / 12th Field Brigade R.A. } Tie |
| 1935 | Mr Hamilton-Russell | The Royals | R.A. Meerut |
| 1936 | Captain Tuck | R.A. | 12th Field Brigade R.A. |
| 1937 | Mr Branford | R.A. | 17/21st Lancers |
| 1938 | Mr Keighly | 19th Lancers | No competition |

* No rains, no cover, no cup.

started would last for 150 years, and that in a single season over four hundred spears in more than thirty tent clubs would hunt the pig in places as far apart as the jungles round Calcutta and the deserts of Hyderabad in Sind. It attracted men from every branch of the services, civil and military, and civilians from all walks of life. One and all, they thought it the finest sport in the world; and the qualities it demanded and developed stood them in good stead in the professions they followed. Philip Woodruff writes of it in *The Men who ruled India:*

> 'The game of games, easily the first in the estimation of all who practised it, was pigsticking. To be good after pig a man must be a horseman, a great asset to a district officer. And he must also have the same qualities—the power of quick but cool judgment, a stout heart, a controlled but fiery ardour and a determination not to be beaten—that are needed in the crisis of a riot, or for that matter for a battle.
>
> 'The kind of man who has those qualities needs to exercise them, the danger and the excitement, the ferocity thus harmlessly given an output, sweetened men who might otherwise have been soured by files and hot weather and disappointment, as lime sweetens grass soured by poultry.
>
> 'Pigsticking and shooting did take a man among the villagers and in fact good pigstickers were usually very good officers.'

# THE RIFLE

# 6. The Jungle

*Camp at Goomur Tal, September 1864*

The army officer in India was entitled to two months' leave every year; his men went off to their villages, and most regimental officers were able to take it. It may sound over generous, but something more than benevolence on the part of authority lay behind it. The object was to give a break from the strain of working shorthanded under the exacting conditions of the Indian hot weather. Looking back, it is remarkable that some well-meaning doctor in Army Headquarters did not press for a rule that leave must be spent at an altitude of not less than 5,000 feet, but luckily no one thought of it. A number of officers did, in fact, take themselves off to shoot or fish in Chamba, Kashmir or beyond, but odd though it may seem, there were plenty who were happy to spend their leave, at any time from March till the monsoon broke in June, in the jungles of the United or Central Provinces, where it was little cooler than it would be when they got back to their regiments to face three months of inferno before mid-September brought some slight relief.

It must be realised that the easy-going days of the Nimrods are now over. The change probably set in about 1880, with the introduction of the Game Laws, but the sportsman in the last fifty years, up to 1947, was faced with totally different conditions. Game, though not scarce as it is today, was no longer plentiful and was generally sought in government-controlled forests where blocks were allotted by permit that laid down the numbers of each species that might be shot. And except for the privileged few, elephants were no longer available. The ordinary man moving about in the jungle, went on his own flat feet. The consequences are predictable. The sportsman worked harder for what he got, and not only in terms of physical effort; personal skill, knowledge and perseverance were all-important. The consequence of that again was that he probably set greater store by what he did get, and as a final dividend he learned to appreciate the infinite charm of the scene on which he was an intruder.

'Pan is not dead, but of all the classic hierarchy survives in triumph; goat-footed, with a gleeful and angry look, the type of the shaggy world; and in every wood, if you go with a spirit properly prepared, you shall hear the sound of his pipe.' So wrote Robert Louis Stevenson. There is a feeling about being alone in the jungle that is hard to put on paper. Born of atavistic memory, it has to date fortunately defied civilisation. It has come down from distant ancestors, whose home was in the jungle and who had for ever to be on the watch for animals larger than they were, equipped with teeth and claws, animals against whose attack a primitive club was not much defence. And with that memory comes the hunting instinct, which has persisted for centuries after man had any need to hunt to win the food he ate or the skins he wore.

There is little evidence that those who went after big game in the years of plenty worried much about the number of animals they shot, but more recently one finds expressed again and again the sentiment that it was not the pleasure of taking life that gave satisfaction, but the sense of achievement at having outwitted the cunning of the wild animal. The hunting instinct was the driving force: it had the upper hand when you were young, conscience pricked more sharply with advancing years.

The physical surroundings are easier to describe. Wherever your fancy took you, they would be in complete contrast with what you had left behind: the set pattern of prim cantonment gardens, the monotonous similarity of the villages of the plains. The word 'jungle' embraces everything from dense tropical forest to thick-scrub-covered hills, and in a country the size of India there was great variety. Here is Burton, in *Sport and Wild Life in the Deccan*, the territory south of the Narbadda river:

> 'The forest was beautiful beyond description. Giant trees, the growth of ages, stood on the river bank, their topmost branches

dotted with vultures and their nests. The river flowed a serpentine course in a rocky bed strewn with great boulders leaving long reaches where crocodiles lay like logs upon the surface and otters disported themselves in pursuit of fish. Sometimes the stream narrowed to a silver thread through stretches of sand, or murmured over pebbly shallows. On its margin, kept green by perennial moisture, grew great brakes of cane and grass jungle. Graceful bamboos bowed their feathery branches to the water. Beyond the level the hillsides were thickly grown with teak and other trees. Shady nullahs containing here and there a pool of water wound their way to join the river.'

North of the Narbadda were the forests of the Central Provinces that Best, the famous forest officer, knew and loved so well. He writes in *Forest Life in India:*

'Even in that season of hot dry air when most of the trees were mere skeletons, naked in their leaflessness, it was lovely. Hill forests have an attraction of their own which appeals with a special charm; there is more mystery about them than there is in the dead level of the plains. There is a greater variety in the vegetation; little glades at the bottom of the valleys; here a mass of bamboos reaching down from the upper slopes, farther on a patch of high forest; round the corner of huge black rocks one would suddenly come on a blazing mass of Butea in full bloom rivalling the sun in brilliance.'

Entering the sal forests, the scenery changed. Much of the contrast was due to the frosts which each winter killed off the yearly growth.

'The general effect is beautiful beyond words, the long valleys flanked by green slopes lead the eye over the sea of thickly packed, stunted shrubs, the sun shining on the young leaves. Poplar-like sal trees stand as sentinels over it all, some forming little promontories into the valley where slightly higher ground runs from the sides of the hills half-way across the lower ground. The picture of these verdant valleys is framed by dark walls of the high forest along the edge of the hills.'

Equally refreshing was the encounter with unspoilt villagers, to many of whom the sight of a white face was a novelty; different again were the aboriginal tribes who lived in the hills of the Central

Provinces, the Deccan and Madras. Gouldsbury, *Tiger Slayer by Order*, met

> 'a party of Karku women swinging down a winding mountain path, armlets and anklets jangling, laughing, a bunch of clematis stuck artistically behind an ear or garlanding a supple leg or arm, a refreshing sight after the prudery of their Hindu sisters of the plains.'

Tribe differed from tribe, but they had much in common. They were superstitious, thriftless, simple, honest and faithful. They would regard you as someone to be amused, laughed with and trusted: a bit of a joke, perhaps, but a real friend if they turned to you in trouble. It was an education just to watch them, to see a Ghond make a fire with two pieces of bamboo and a pinch of dry tree cotton. It goes without saying that you made full use of the knowledge and skill they so willingly offered you. Powell dedicates *Call of The Tiger* to 'his three Indian shikaris, Darbari, Saktu and Abhu, without whose help and friendship my earlier efforts would surely have been in vain'. Burton had a friend called Indru.

> 'In this country I found Indru, a Ghond hunter of primeval type living in a thatched bamboo hovel. He was captured with difficulty. The Shikaris who went on ahead said the Ghonds were so timid that if they went to the door of the hut the occupant would escape by the back, if both front and back were guarded he would force his way out through the roof. Indru had never set eyes on a white man although he was close on seventy years of age, still he came to me fearlessly and sat at my feet where a tot of rum put him quite at his ease. He was grizzled and wrinkled and of a somewhat simian cast of countenance and altogether an uninviting aspect to the superficial observer, but I saw in him a mighty hunter looking with fearless eyes, of few words and direct speech. He was armed with an old matchlock and had a powder flask made from the horn of a gazelle which must have been very old for it was worn quite smooth.'

In *The Lonely Tiger*, Hugh Allen writes of one he knew.

> 'He was as brave as any man I have ever met. He was a Chenchu—the name by which the aboriginal jungle man of these areas is known—and he carried a bow and a quiver of arrows

> like most Chenchus do. These and a filthy rag as a loincloth were apparently his only possessions. One thing more he had, and I think it was his greatest asset. Appu, for that was his name, had a most infectious smile and a marvellous sense of humour.'

In most places the jungle teemed with life, creatures that walked or stalked, crawled or flew. How much you saw and heard depended on how much you knew what to look and listen for. Sometimes a red-letter day would come your way as it did for a man who set out to stalk a tiger lying in a pool in the heat of the day, and wrote an article for *The Field*.

> 'Other of the local jungle folk put in an appearance. A white breasted kingfisher was seated on a rock a few yards from the pool, then sweeping close over the tiger's back he neatly picked a minnow from the side of the sleeping monster and carried it to a branch across the pool. From the branch he again swooped into the pool and up over the tiger on to the rock from which he had started. During the whole period of the stalk the kingfisher continued his fishing. A grey jungle cock walked calmly across the nullah thirty or forty yards from the tiger and a little later a pair of spur fowls picked their way daintily across, a bare twenty paces from the little pool. Neither jungle fowl nor spur fowl paid the least attention to the great feline. Then a peahen appeared to drink and was vastly perturbed to find the tiger laying slumbering in the middle of the pool. For half an hour she perambulated within twenty paces of the tiger continually uttering a tock-tock of disgust. Each tock was uttered at a distinct interval, indicating in jungle language that there was danger by the pool, but not such as to call for hurried flight. Very different is the peafowl's call of tok-tok-tok-tok-tok in rapid succession, indicating immediate danger and the need for urgent action. Several times the peahen advanced to the very edge of the pool, and twice her head went down to drink when she can have been no more than four paces from the tiger, but her courage failed and as she drank it cannot have been more than the most hurried sip. By now I was little more than sixty yards from the tiger. All had gone well with the stalk. By carefully watching the tiger's head I had time to freeze as he raised it and before his gaze turned in my direction. I had marked a comfortable rock two moves ahead. Once on this I could either wait for the tiger to rise, which he was likely to do very soon, or make a slight noise to arouse him, with rifle at the shoulder and finger on the trigger. I

> had however made one fatal blunder. The peafowl is perhaps the most sharp-sighted and wary of the jungle folk. Intent on the tiger I had failed to take account of the danger of being spotted by the peahen. I was in the middle of almost the last move, rifle across the knees, weight of the body raised off the ground on both hands, when loud and clear rang out the signal, tok-tok-tok-tok-tok, that conveys an instant warning to all jungle folk within hearing. Up came the tiger's head, sensing instinctively the direction from which danger threatened, and by the time my rifle had reached my shoulder he had disappeared into the jungle. A snapshot might have been taken but was not. As the tiger made off a couple of raucous grunts from a treetop indicated the presence of a troop of langurs. As long as the tiger lay quiet they had given no sound and only gave tongue when he moved.
>
> 'The stalk had failed. For two hours I had had the tiger before me and I had let him go without pressing the trigger. I could not regret his escape. The intimate view of home life in the jungle that I enjoyed is a memory worth many tiger skins.'

There were a few animals that sooner or later would certainly be seen, even by the less observant. The jackal, or at any rate the unmistakable cry he makes, is familiar throughout the length and breadth of India. His call is a long wailing howl repeated on a higher scale three or four times and ending with three yelps. They generally go about in pairs, but may collect in packs to hunt the smaller deer. To hear them then in full cry, strident, staccato, snivelling, echoing their leader, is like listening to a 'chorus of the tortured in an opera of the damned'.

The single jackal has been known, in the role that has made his name a household word, to act as hanger-on to a tiger. 'Cheeky, intelligent, adaptable and insignificant', he has nothing to fear and is probably tolerated as providing another pair of ears and eyes to give warning of impending danger.

The wild dog is the cleverest of all the hunters, and the implacable enemy of everything that lives in the jungle. For that reason he was regarded as vermin and shot without compunction. Their relations towards man were peculiar. There is no evidence that they ever killed a human being, but they were extraordinarily bold and inquisitive. A pack might stand and gaze, even after one of them had been shot. Towards the domestic dog their attitude was even more curious. They were more than a match for even a savage and powerful pack, but if your dogs were too small to be aggressive they might approach and attempt to fraternise; fawning, gambolling and trying to play with them.

Once a pack of wild dogs scents or sees a deer its fate is sealed. They hunt mercilessly and with intelligence, and they fear neither man nor beast. Kenneth Anderson in *The Tiger Roars* describes how he watched them deal with a tiger that killed a sambhur stag they were pursuing. The stag in headlong flight almost literally collided with the tiger, who killed it before he realised what was happening. The pack arrived hot on its heels. The tiger stood to defend his kill but they would have none of it. There were nine of them and in a flash they surrounded him. The bird-like hunting cry of a moment earlier changed abruptly to a chorus of long, plaintive notes. They were calling up reinforcements, and every dog within hearing would answer the call.

The tiger rose to face them. His face contorted with rage, he snarled and roared defiance, but the nervous twitching of his tail betrayed his feelings of doubt and fear. The dogs stood fast, legs firmly yet slightly outspread. The tiger, realising that time was on the side of his enemies, charged the nearest dog facing him. It side-stepped and its comrades closed in to attack from behind. The tiger whirled round flaying wildly with its forepaws which struck one dog on its hindquarters, almost severing a leg. As its body was flung in the air the dogs behind tore chunks from his heaving flanks. He swung round again and two more dogs were torn asunder, but he lost his advantage by pausing to bury his fangs in the body nearest him. Dogs from all sides now swarmed over him tearing out scraps of living flesh. By a supreme effort he freed himself, but as he did so a new sound was heard above the pandemonium: the cry of the reinforcements. The tiger heard and the fight went out of him. He turned tail and fled, the surviving six dogs in hot pursuit.

First three dogs reached the scene, then another and another. A brief pause to sniff the bloodstained grass and they raced off in fury in the wake of the hunt. A minute later a pack of nearly a dozen arrived, paused, and rushed off to join the others. The tiger's fate was sealed. They would not give up till they had torn him to pieces.

The *bandar log* of Kipling's *Jungle Book* were the Bengal monkeys, medium sized, with brown hair, a short tail and a red behind, 'mischievous, unlovely and unlovable'. In the jungle they were usually found in the vicinity of some old ruined fort where their ancestors had lived when the place was inhabited by some long-forgotten petty chieftain.

The other monkey commonly met was langur, a large handsome animal with a fine long tail, a beautiful greyish coat, black face and hands. They move in troops of a dozen or more under the leadership of an old male and were a great help to sportsmen as they seldom let tiger or panther pass without giving notice of its whereabouts. They were extremely active and crossed immense gaps between trees, bounding and swinging from one branch to the next with split-second accuracy of timing and distance.

Last and least of the jungle folk was one against whose anger, if provoked, there was no defence: the bees. It was wiser to avoid them. There was a locality noted for its panthers and its black bees, and it was said that the panthers were the less dangerous of the two.

There is the memory of stepping out on to a balcony of an old Rajput fort and coming unpleasantly face to face with a bees' nest, a sinister, black, inverted cone: and the memory of being buzzed, escorted firmly and unmistakably by a single bee down to the main gateway. Others were not so lucky. The sportsman who figures in the next chapter, in the story of the tigress with the black collar, decided to have a look at the cave that had been her lying-up place. His friend pleaded that the climb down into the nullah was too much for his sprained ankle so he went alone with a villager to act as guide.

> 'The cave was large and roomy. At the far end a spring of pure water splashed down the rocks and above it, hanging from the roof, was a huge nest of jungle bees: dark and ominous, a great inverted cone about five feet deep. I hung back nervously, but before I could stop him the villager decided to have a drink at the spring. Things then happened very quickly. The nest exploded like a bomb and the bees were on us. The man draped himself in the dirty white sheet he was carrying and vanished out of the cave like a demented ghost. Wearing only a bush shirt and shorts I had nothing to cover me. Advice I had heard flashed through my mind as I tore handfuls of bees from my face and neck. "Lie flat on the floor, they will soon tire of stinging you." But lying flat on the floor of that gloomy cave, with the nest still erupting above, did not seem the answer. I fled after the ghost, squashing handfuls of bees as I went. "Throw yourself into the water." But those swirling, rocky pools looked most uninviting. I stumbled blindly on, then a figure loomed up: it was my orderly. He handed me the branch of a tree and we fought a rearguard action, flaying the air like windmills.'

He managed to cover the three miles back to the bungalow where the forest ranger produced an old man, famed as a bee wizard. He started pulling out the stings, all the time making a low buzzing sound like the hum of distant bees. The effect was most soothing and before long the victim announced that, given half an hour's rest, he would be fit to take part in the feast they had planned to celebrate the death of the tigress. But it was a vain boast: his meal that evening was a glass of milk. After a wretched, sleepless night, when dawn broke he crawled to his mirror and lifting an eyelid peered at what was left of his face. 'I seemed to have no eyes or neck at all and vaguely resembled a sloth bear.'

It was not until he had spent several days in bed that he fully recovered.

'Anyway,' said his friend helpfully, 'you'll never suffer from rheumatism.'

# 7. Tigers

*A Critical Moment*

In regulating the level of game in government forests, with due regard to the lives and livelihood of the inhabitants of the bordering villages, the tiger was the key figure. 'Tigers must prey', says Shakespeare, and that was the crux of the matter. Pig and deer were the animals that were most destructive to crops and, particularly the deer, they were the natural food of the tiger. If there were enough tigers, damage to crops would be held at a reasonable level. There were two things the government was able to do to maintain the balance. The forest officer, when issuing game permits, regulated the number of tigers that might be shot, and the district officer restricted the number of licences granted to villagers to possess firearms for crop protection. Given a free hand, they would have decimated the smaller game and the tiger would have started taking cattle: and a cattle killer, if only because he can so easily become a man-eater, is a greater scourge than whole herds of deer. He can cause complete communities to desert their villages and move away. In the mid 1860s, the heyday of the years of plenty, tigers in Bengal alone were killing over 2,000 men a year and there were neighbourhoods where it was a question of whether tiger or man would prevail: and sometimes the tiger won.

Most animals in captivity, however cleverly contrived their surroundings, are but pale shadows of their natural selves, and none suffers more in this respect than the tiger. The spots, the stripes and irregular patches of black which contrast strongly with the back-

*Gliding like a Phantom*

ground colouring are designed to distort and conceal; in captivity they have if anything the opposite effect. Nor can there be any true appreciation of the true glory of the background, 'the tints varying from every shade of pale yellow, to ochre, to deep golden red and burnt sienna'. The paces possible within the confines of a cage do not even hint at the silent gliding walk of the tiger in his natural surroundings. 'He seems to flow past one like a phantom.' This impression is created partly by the silent tread, but even more by the action. The limbs on the same side move together and it is this that produces the gliding effect. The proud insolent stare, challenging the intruder in the jungle to explain his presence, gives way in captivity to a look of unutterable boredom.

Sher Jung in *Tryst with Tigers* describes how as a boy he was given a new rifle and went out to shoot a peacock. His dog was seized by an uncontrollable fit of shivering. He followed its gaze and:

> 'saw a huge figure standing head-on and foreshortened in the wan light of the setting sun—the cause of the dog's discountenance. It looked like a beautiful frieze to me, painted on the wall of the opaque evening.
>
> 'The figure paused for a while, superimposing the gold and black of its coat on the gold and black extravaganza of the dusk; then, head slung low and body arched, it glided forward into the bed of the stream. For a moment I failed to recognise it, the only thing my mind registered was the rhythmical grace of its walk and the smooth outline of its body. The figure gained the middle of the *Khol*, and only then did the realisation flash across my mind that it was a tiger.
>
> 'It walked straight to the pool near us, stood for a while, looked round, and then, slowly and gracefully, like a sun-flecked cloud, it lowered its body and dipped its whiskered face into the calm of the pool.
>
> 'The tiger took a long time to drink its fill, and I had a whole age to myself of the rarest spectacle the earth can offer. Then like a vision it rose to its full height, shook its massive head, and with the water dripping from its lower lip, disappeared into the dusk.'

There is nothing lanky about the tiger. He is a large, powerful, burly animal, differing entirely in his wild state from the impression one gets from looking at him in captivity. He is immensely powerful and with a single blow from his paw can crack a man's skull like an eggshell; but he is not clumsy. He can clear a ravine in an effortless leap of thirty feet from bank to bank; and a tigress has been seen to drag the body of a half-grown bullock up a river bank without apparent effort. The bank was of alluvial soil and so steep that a man would have had to use his hands to climb it.

The tiger has a stable temperament and when picked up as cubs they have been kept as pets till nearly a year old. One keen animal lover, who was by implication a bachelor, records that if well fed they are neither treacherous nor likely to show any sudden savageness. He 'had one of considerable size that used to be loose in my room at night, and though I pillowed it and thumped it, when it would show its affection for me by jumping on the bed as soon as I was asleep, it never showed any resentment.'

The tiger has nothing to fear from any other animal in the jungle, and from the extreme caution he shows when returning to the carcase of an animal he has killed, particularly if he has any reason to suspect human interference, one can only assume that he learns with his mother's milk that man is the enemy, to be avoided if possible. If he has had no direct contact with man and is not emotionally upset, he will go out of his way to avoid a meeting. There is the memory of approaching a buffalo that had been tied up at a point where the dry bed of a stream cut through a high bank that formed the boundary between the forest and the open grass-land below. The animal was found lying on its side, struggling to regain its feet. There was not a scratch on it, but imprinted in the sand were the pug marks of a tiger that must have passed that way only a few seconds earlier. He had heard man coming and thought it wiser to look elsewhere for his dinner.

On a chance encounter a tiger will express his disapproval with no uncertain voice, but he will give ground and vanish into the jungle. On the other hand, if for any reason his temper has been ruffled, anything can happen and extreme caution is necessary. The first and obvious cause for an upset is a wound or injury, recent or of long standing. Again, if there is known to be a tigress with cubs in the locality it is only prudent to be careful, though the maternal instinct is less strongly developed than in the panther. She may defend her young, but more often fear overcomes affection and she will slink off.

Under the emotional stress of the mating season the behaviour of both male and female can be totally unpredictable. Hugh Allen tells how he went with a shotgun and a handful of cartridges to shoot a peafowl for the pot and came across a large panther apparently asleep stretched out on the sand of a nullah. But a closer look showed that it was dead and that a small part of the hindquarters had been eaten. On the other side of a fallen tree he came across the body of a huge wild boar. The mask was set in a ferocious snarl and one tusk was stained brown with congealed blood. The body had been terribly ripped and torn but very little had been eaten. This was the work of a tiger, and if the blood-stained tusk meant anything the tiger had not had the fight all its own way. As he rose from examining the boar he realised the jungle was strangely quiet.

Suddenly, without warning, a tiger appeared only five yards away. It did not at first see him as it was moving obliquely away, but some slight start caused it to stop and turn. He then saw that it was a tigress and that she was looking straight at him. But the eyes were vacant and unseeing. She turned and disappeared into nearby cover. He saw that she was plastered with dried mud and that along her left flank ran a long bloody gash; and she was moving with a marked limp.

He was about to follow her when he looked down and realised that he was carrying a shotgun with number six in the left barrel and buckshot in the right. He was fumbling in his pocket for a lethal ball when with a terrific roar the tigress once more shot into view and with a mighty bound landed in the clearing some thirty paces away. The surprise was so complete that he dropped the ball cartridge, and that perhaps saved his life, as if he had fired before he had had time to grasp what was going on there would have been no hope for him. A more careful look showed that the animal in front of him was not the tigress but a tiger, bent on mischief. There began a terrifying display of feint attacks punctuated by loud roars. The animal would rush in then check with lips bared in a vicious snarl. He would leap sideways then start weaving and roaring again. The real attack could not be long delayed. He was wondering whether he should snap shut the gun and try for its head with the buckshot in the right barrel when the cause of all the trouble became clear. He saw the tigress sitting under a small tree like a big cat in front of the fire. On her face was a pleased smile as she watched what was going on. The two were mating, which explained her behaviour of a few minutes earlier, for it is not uncommon for a female in season to go about in a kind of dazed ecstatic trance. There was no trance about the tiger. He was out for business. The encounter was just what he wanted, a chance to show off.

Help came from an unexpected quarter. A storm had been brewing and suddenly a thin tongue of violet lightning flickered down in a brilliant flash. There was a deafening crash of thunder, then in a solid sheet of water the rain came cascading down. The tiger gave up. The rain rattling and bouncing off his back drove the ardour out of him. He wheeled and trotted away with the tigress bounding after him.

And there is on record the story of a tiger and tigress who by way of whetting their appetite for their love-making took on and between them killed a nearly full-grown elephant.

A tigress matures at the age of four, and over the next fifteen years may produce 15–20 cubs, born two or three at a time at three-yearly intervals. A simple sum shows that by the end of her useful life her offspring will be numbered in hundreds. The numbers had therefore to be kept down, and as the tiger reigned supreme in the jungle, only by carefully regulated shooting could this be done.

## TIGERS

Tiger shooting is not a sport to be embarked on lightly. You must know how to set about it, the habits of the beast, the precautions you must take. You need the right sort of rifle, firing suitable ammunition, and in a tropical climate you must make sure that both are in perfect condition. You must have confidence in your marksmanship. There must be a heavily odds-on chance of hitting, and hitting in the spot you aim at. When things go well there is an element of danger that lends spice to any sport, mountaineering or motor racing, but no more than that. But if things go wrong it is likely, one way or another, to be your fault. If the tiger gets away wounded the risks multiply enormously and not only your own life but the lives of those with you are in danger. You start all over again and the odds are no longer in your favour.

There are two ways of bringing a tiger on to the sights of your rifle, each with its alternative. You can go to look for him, either on the back of an elephant or on foot; or you can sit and wait for him to come to you, either of his own free will to finish eating an animal he has killed or because you have made a plan to drive him up to where you are sitting.

Shooting from an elephant was all very well in the good old days when you could hire one as easily as a hansom cab in Piccadilly, but from the turn of the present century, at any rate in the United and Central Provinces, the only people likely to have elephants at their disposal were the large landowners, forest officers and commissioners of districts. If you were stationed there and had influential friends that was one thing, but for the ordinary person coming on leave from the Punjab or beyond they could be ruled out. Assam was an exception. Wild elephants were plentiful and provided a source of supply of tame animals that could be hired from villagers.

By comparison with other methods there was not the same scope for jungle craft, for pitting your wits against those of the tiger. The man in charge of the proceedings made a plan, the rest sat tight and hoped they would be lucky enough to get a shot; though perhaps sit tight is not quite the right word. The ordinary howdah is not designed for shooting from; it is hard to get an all-round view and swing a rifle. The whole thing needs a lot of practice, and anything can happen if elephant or mahout, or both, lose their nerve when the tiger appears. There is an account in the *Royal Artillery Journal* of a shoot in Assam. There were four guns, and on the first day they had had some sport so the whole countryside heard of their arrival and crowded in to see the tigers and the strange sahibs who had come to shoot them: also in the hope of getting some tiger fat, a sovereign remedy for rheumatism.

The next day a tiger was located in an area of grass and a plan was made. It was a quaint scene. Trees were few and the jungle fairly open, so everybody had a good view of the proceedings. The countryside was well populated and one and all had been waiting for some hours for the show to begin. Hundreds of spectators had collected and were manning all available trees to see the fun. As soon as the elephants entered the grass the tiger began to move and there ensued such a yelling and cheering from all sides that it was pretty clear that the chances of getting a shot were very small. It was hardly surprising that the tiger broke the wrong way and escaped in the darkness.

It was good fun while it lasted and if you were lucky enough to get a shot, but it was not a very satisfying way of spending two months' leave.

Tiger shooting on foot is the most exciting method of all. You might be lucky and just meet one when your paths crossed, as you and he were about your more or less lawful occasions. Then, provided you lived up to the old adage 'thrice armed is he who gets his blow in fust', it was all too easy. But for what was in effect stalking a tiger it was essential to reconnoitre carefully and weigh up all the relevant factors: where to find him, how to approach him and what he was likely to do if you did not get a shot, or if he got away wounded. Your line of approach should not coincide with his likely line of retreat.

Much depended on the time of year. In the cold weather tigers were on the move all day, the grass was long and the visibility poor, and the only chance was to stalk the spot where you had tied your bait, chosen to give you a favourable approach, in the hope of finding the tiger on the kill, which had been tied securely to prevent him dragging it away. In the hot weather things were different. There was far less cover, the tiger would lie up during the day, and water was so scarce that the isolated jungle pool was the key point. The bait was tied a few hundred yards from the water, which you stalked in the heat of the day in the hope of finding the tiger asleep.

If you decided to wait for the tiger to come to you there were two schools of thought: those who favoured beating, the dry-fly fishermen, inclined to look down on their less skilful brethren, the sitters-up or the chuck-and-chance-it brigade. There was something to be said for both sides. It was a matter of fancy waistcoats, of weighing up the means at your disposal and the respective chances of success.

The beater would argue that there was no guarantee that a tiger would of his own free will return to the kill, and that sitting up often involved shooting after dark, which was an unsatisfactory business likely to result in missing or wounding. The organisation of a beat, on the other hand, called for much experience of the habits of tigers and a careful study of the ground, and if all went according to plan was far more likely to succeed. The sitter-up would reply that of the two, his was the more testing battle of wits: to persuade a tiger, that most suspicious of beasts, to return to a kill where someone was lying in wait for him. There was considerable skill in choosing the exact place and great demands were made on patience, nerves and self-control.

Whichever method you choose, you had first to locate a tiger in an area small enough for you to make a plan to bring him to terms. If you were lucky enough to find the carcase of an animal, wild or domestic, that the tiger had killed of his own accord, fair enough, so long as the indications were that he would come back for a second meal. The alternative was to tempt him with a bait of your own providing, usually a young buffalo tied up at a spot he was likely to pass when questing for game. Such a practice may seem to break every canon of British regard for fair play and, looked at out of context, it does seem a trifle mean to leave a poor defenceless beast at the mercy of the first tiger to come along. But there was more to it than that. A tiger must prey, and if the one you were trying to locate did not kill your buffalo he killed something else. Moreover, up to the last moment the animal remained in blissful ignorance of its impending fate. The tiger is a most efficient engine of destruction and those who have seen one kill testify to 'being awed by its ruthlessness and savage ferocity, the lustful pleasure taken in killing its prey'.

A beat that brought a tiger up to the point where you sat with your rifle waiting for him was the culmination of a lot of hard work, based on a shrewd appreciation of the animal's likely behaviour in that particular setting. The commissioner of the Kumaon referred to in Chapter 1 had long given up shooting himself, but it was his practice to invite to his Christmas camp four or five friends less fortunate than he. The beat each day would be planned to drive the tiger up to a line of rifles, but one man would be told that it would probably come out in front of him and that he had better make the most of his opportunity, as next day he would be less well placed. That such a forecast could be made was due to the fact that a tiger awakened by beaters and actuated by fear of man will follow a path that can be foretold with some accuracy from a knowledge of the lie of the land and of the habits of tigers generally. He can be persuaded to take that path, but the beat is likely to fail if it attempts to force him to do what he would not naturally do, such as move into the open or cross a space devoid of cover.

The object of tying up a bait as a preliminary to a beat was no more than to locate a tiger in a suitable area. There had to be cover nearby into which he could drag his kill and, preferably uphill, a pool of water located in cover where he could sleep after he had eaten and drunk his fill.

The kill would be visited not too early next morning, to do no more than confirm from the marks of the drag that the tiger had taken it in the right direction. That established, planning could begin. The less coming and going in the vicinity of a sleeping tiger the better, so you would have reconnoitred the ground the day before. It was always worth while consulting local opinion, which might well come up with a plan adopted by one 'Makanji Sahib' who had shot a tiger there way back in 1908. Every detail would have been handed down from father to son, invested with all the sanctity of the law and the prophets, but before accepting it blind it was advisable to check that conditions, such as the time of year, the cover and the water, were still the same.

The simplest layout for a beat was a rough triangle. The stops formed the sides, the beaters the base, while the rifles were at the apex. The stops tapped gently if the tiger showed any sign of straying from the path you intended for him. It was an important job for which you chose the most intelligent, and told them exactly what to do. A premature tap might ruin the whole beat. You had also to arrange a signal to the beaters to take to the trees if things went wrong and a dangerous situation developed.

And that things could go wrong is recalled by two faded snapshots that fluttered out of an old dictionary. One of them shows a group of villagers at the foot of a tree in a clearing in the jungle. In the centre stands a British officer on leave from one of the Frontier Militias, by his side his Khattak orderly, looking as always 'like a debonair bandit'. Against the tree, which is branchless to its first fork, stands a roughly made ladder. The other photo is a close-up of the trunk showing a spot about nine feet up. The bark is scored as though by innumerable sword cuts.

The story behind the photo emphasises that something more than a knowledge of jungle lore may be required of the sportsman who sets out to shoot a tiger.

Two young officers had left Waziristan in high spirits, bound for a block in the Central Provinces. 'We'll bag a couple of tigers each in the first fortnight and then buzz off to Kashmir.' Visions of a houseboat on the Wular as a base for days after trout or maybe a couple of large mahseer from the lake itself.

They were met on arrival at their forest bungalow by a ranger, who introduced himself as a keen shikari. There were, he said, at least three tigers in the block and he had already bought young buffaloes to tie as baits. The next couple of days passed in reconnaissance. No shooting, it was to be tigers or nothing. One animal was known to the villagers as it had killed an old woman who had stumbled across it while gathering firewood. It was reputed to have a large black mane.

Then came the day when one of the baits was killed. It had been tied on top of the bank of a nullah, precipitous, rocky and deep, and the body had been dragged and hauled over the edge to fall at the mouth of the cave where the tiger's lay up. An ideal spot for a beat, said the ranger. It was in the bag. He seemed to know every inch of the way and led them downstream to a spot where they would sit in trees, one on either bank. He pointed out in passing other trees in which stops would be posted, but seemed to think they were of little importance as the sides of the nullah were so steep that no tiger in its senses would attempt to climb them. The ranger went off to collect the beaters. This took time and it was well on in the afternoon before going on his way had sprung up the tree where the first stop started. Rifles were swung, sights aligned on likely spots, the shouts came nearer, rose to a crescendo; then came two shots from a 12-bore: a deathly silence, followed by a confused babbling. The ranger had been lent the gun and had placed himself near one of the stops and it seemed as though he had fired in an attempt to prevent the tiger breaking out. They hurried to the spot and found that the tiger had indeed broken out. He had climbed out of the nullah and before going on his way had sprung up the trees where the first stop was posted. The man was still there astride a branch, a measured seventeen feet above the ground. The tree was on a flat grassy spot well clear of the bank so that the tiger had had no high ground from which to spring; but that was what he had done. At a height of nine feet the trunk was scarred by claw marks, and though it seemed incredible that he could have done so, he had made the extra few feet and reached the man's leg which was hanging down.

With the help of a roughly made ladder they lowered him to the ground. His left leg was a terrible sight, pulped from the knee downwards. He was carried to the bungalow and made as comfortable as possible and a young clerk from the forest post sent off on a bicycle to fetch the nearest doctor, the civil surgeon in Narsinghpur, eighteen miles away.

In the mind of one of those two officers—who is still alive today—the memory of the next few hours is like a bad dream. The long, hot evening wore on, but the doctor did not arrive. At last they could bear it no longer, and he set off himself, accompanied by his orderly carrying a canvas bag of drinking water, for there was cholera in all the villages around. They arrived in the small hours of the morning after an exhausting trip and found the doctor asleep under a mosquito-proof cage surrounded by the beds of his numerous family. He had received the message, but had not appreciated its urgency. The injured man was eventually got to hospital but although he had made an apparently good recovery immediately after the attack, he died of secondary shock following an operation.

Kashmir disappeared over the horizon. Just one thought consumed them; to shoot the tiger that had done the damage. Another bait was tied, killed and dragged at exactly the same spot. The beat ran on the same lines except that they sat in trees nearer the kill, but the tiger broke out at the same place and as there was no stop in the fateful tree it once again escaped.

The cholera epidemic was getting serious and every village was now infected. An arch of branches appeared at the entrance to the nearest hamlet, erected to encourage the pestilence to depart and make its way elsewhere. There was no talk now of 'a brace apiece', one tiger, the tiger, was all they wanted. They tramped for miles, morning and evening, through the arid jungles visiting their baits. They planned a great feast and kept choice tinned delicacies to celebrate his death. Nothing happened, then at long last, when they were seriously thinking they would have to move, the tiger killed again: the same place, the same method. They cut through the pack for the ace of spades, the winner to take his place in a tree covering the spot where the tiger had broken out; the loser to sit a hundred yards away covering the nullah.

> '"S" drew the black ace, and that was that. The beat started as usual and shortly afterwards I heard the crack of his rifle. Then I heard my orderly shout, "The sahib has killed it". I found him throwing wood apples at the tiger lying at the foot of his tree, "just to make sure it was dead".'

It turned out to be a young tigress of no great size but in perfect condition. The stripes around her neck were so placed that at certain angles it did look as though she was wearing a black horse collar. But the great feast was indefinitely postponed: in the hour of triumph they had trouble with the bees.

On the other hand if things went well for you and you were on your own, success was a tonic to the jaded spirit.

## TIGERS

From the *Field:*

'It was with a feeling of great content that I turned in that first night. In the morning I had sat at my office table wading through ponderous files and dreading the arrival of some untoward news that might prevent my jungle trip. Then came forty miles by motor and a ten-mile ride in the cool of a December evening. As I lay on my little camp cot the darkness of the jungle rose like a wall a bare fifty yards from the tent, shutting out the cares of a heavy district. Far, far away was the chattering of Gandhi and his disciples. The starry sky was overhead and the sounds and smells of the jungle were around me.

'The place selected for the sit up was a rather nasty bit of jungle. Up to a height of six feet from the ground was a mass of bare stems the thickness of a man's wrist, and above that a twisted, matted tangle of branches and foliage would render it impossible to shoot except from the ground. Even so, it was necessary to cut and remove all the stems in order to obtain two narrow lines of fire, one running down towards the nullah, the other at an angle of forty-five to my front. The extreme width of the jungle at this point was not over fifty yards and if all went well it seemed that the tiger could scarcely fail to pass within easy shot.

'The beat started with the usual discordant din of tom-toms and shouting, and the beaters came along all too slowly as it seemed to my impatient ear. They were now approaching and it seemed as if the beat were blank after all when a peafowl arose with a great scurry of wings a hundred yards away and flapped noisily overhead. The peafowl is a noisy, heavy bird which seldom cares to fly save when alarmed at the sight of a tiger or panther, which causes it to take wing.

'So the rifle was brought a little nearer to the ready position and I eagerly scanned the jungle before me. It was no false alarm. In another minute the tiger appeared some forty yards ahead and halted for a moment broadside on to gaze in the direction of the nullah. Before the sights could be aligned on his brawny neck, the only portion that was clearly visible, he turned and moved on towards me, softly and noiselessly advancing on a line which would bring him past within a few yards of where I sat. As he emerged on the first line of fire something in my position attracted his attention and he stopped. The heavy rifle had been following his every movement and as the great head turned enquiringly towards me my finger tightened on the trigger.

> Never before had it been my good fortune to have such a front-seat view of the death of a great feline.'

If for any reason a beat was not practicable and it was decided to sit up and wait for the tiger to return to his kill, the actual site at which to tie the bait was then all-important, as it would be the scene of the final encounter.

It should offer the tiger on his return an approach through continuous cover, and should be away from tracks used by villagers. The junction of forest tracks on a small nullah crossing a fireline was an ideal spot. The bait had to be tied firmly by the leg with an unbreakable rope, and no more than thirty yards from the spot in which you were going to sit. This might be in a hollow in a bank, but more usually in a machan tied in a tree. A machan is by definition a platform. Those who shot regularly would carry a country-made bedstead, strung with rope, with the legs sawn off so that it could be lashed into the branches. Alternatives were planks or poles cut and covered with a camp mattress. Unless you had experienced men working for you it was wise to supervise the work yourself. One beginner who, in his ignorance, left it to the local villagers, found on his arrival a platform on which 'he might more fittingly have knelt in prayer, as when he sat on it his legs, dangling down, were less than six feet above the ground'.

A tiger's senses of sight and hearing are acute beyond human comprehension and no detail was too trifling to ensure that at the critical moment you would be able to bring your rifle into your shoulder and align the sights in absolute silence and with the minimum of movement, and without finding that a branch or a length of rope was in the way. In expectation of a long wait a reasonable degree of comfort was essential, and it would be unfortunate, to say the least of it, after your men had gone away, chattering happily to themselves, to find that you were sitting on an ants' nest. But once settled, you had the jungle to yourself. Its inhabitants did not know you were there. Unseen and unsuspected, you might see and hear them go about their business.

But you could get too engrossed in what was going on. Sher Jung relates how from his hideout he had a grandstand view of a small herd of elephants at play in a large pool in the stream below him, spraying one another with mud and water.

> 'Suddenly I felt something nudge me gently on the outer bend of my thigh. I was sitting cross-legged like the Buddha, and my legs were covered with a thin blanket fold. I glanced down

> through the edges of my eyes and to my horror I saw a huge black cobra slithering across my blanket with its head climbing to my thigh . . . I knew that the only possible escape . . . lay in remaining absolutely motionless. I had always admired the sleek beauty of snakes, with their texture of colour and their simplicity of grace. This one was too close for comfort and admiration. . . . .
>
> 'After what seemed virtually ages I felt the absence of weight and friction on my legs. I could not believe it and did not open my eyes . . . At last the pins and needles at the back of my eyelids forced me to open them. There was no snake anywhere around me.'

Sitting up more often than not was a matter of a long night vigil and for those who favoured it this was where the real attraction lay. Not for them the discordant din of tom-toms, the shouting of the beaters. With the stillness of the night there came a peaceful charm, a freshness of air and a quiet of mind that is the special gift of solitude. Never was the charm so potent as when the moon was at its full.

Some of the jungle people believe that there are *deos* (spirits) which move about by night. They cannot be seen or heard, but their presence is felt by animals and human beings alike. When they pass by they impose absolute stillness on all by their occult powers. In *Call of the Tiger*, M. M. Ismail writes:

> 'I have experienced this more than once. The absolute silence is eerie, and one is afraid even to breathe. I remember on one occasion when I must have been dozing this sudden and absolute silence wakened me with a start. My hand went to my rifle but I could not move for a minute or two. I could hear the beating of my own heart, and then just as suddenly everything was normal again. I was not afraid, but by some unknown influence I was compelled to remain absolutely still.'

You might of course sit through the night in vain. The tiger did not return, or he came and his suspicions were aroused by some careless movement on your part and he went away again. Then in the chill light of the dawn you climbed down from your machan, stretched your cramped limbs and made your way back to camp, bath and breakfast. But if you were lucky there would come a sudden climax of sounds. The startled cries of the monkeys and the deer, perhaps even a call from the tiger himself, told you that your vigil was nearly over. The tension was acute.

> 'After a long time he entered the fire line about seventy or eighty yards from me and saw the buffalo. I could see him quite clearly in the moonlight, but it was too long a shot to attempt at night. He crossed the fireline and went into the scrub on the other side. I kept my eyes fixed on the ten yards of open ground between the buffalo and the scrub jungle. I wanted to kill him before he reached the buffalo. There was no noise except once or twice a small twig snapped under the five hundred pounds or more of his massive bulk. Then suddenly, about four paces away from the buffalo, the tiger stood up—as if he had come out of the earth. . . . I had not seen him come out of the scrub though I had not taken my eyes off that place for a moment. In a completely unhurried manner he walked up to the buffalo. I could see only a huge paw on the animal's withers, and just the top of the tiger's massive head on the other side. The rest of his body was concealed. Fortunately just then the buffalo staggered a little and swung round bringing the tiger towards me. With the report of the rifle he collapsed. The heavy 300 grain bullet of the ·375 magnum had severed his spine eight inches behind the base of his skull and going through his neck had gone deep into his chest. He felt no pain and died instantaneously in the moment of victory.'

A tiger returning to a kill was unlikely to do so until the evening and he might in fact come at any hour during the night. The difficulty of shooting in the dark was one of the great disadvantages of sitting-up.

In the government forests of the United Provinces there was a complete ban on night shooting, starting one hour after sunset. It was imposed after an incident in which a party, incompetent and careless, wounded a tiger at night and left to others the task of following up and dealing with it. In areas where night shooting was allowed the phase of the moon was a factor of great importance in siting both bait and machan. If there was no moon you were at a great disadvantage, unless you used an electric torch strapped to your rifle.

A man-eater or persistent cattle killer was a pest and any means were justified in getting rid of it. But for an ordinary tiger where did you draw the line? In *Wild Animals in Central India* Dunbar Brander, forthright as usual, feels that the tiger must be given a sporting chance.

> 'I do not think a torch gives a fair chance and does not call up those qualities in man which we expect him to possess when he hunts a beast like a tiger. One expects endurance, skill, self-possession and a certain amount of courage. . . . If we admit the electric torch at what point do we stop?'

There was yet another way of staging an encounter with a tiger. You could imitate the call of the animal so that it came to you. For those who had scruples over sacrificing a buffalo to achieve their end there was much to be said for it, but it was no game for the beginner. It resolved the issue to a purely personal level: man *v.* tiger, and no holds barred.

To start with, you had to learn how to call. Corbett, with years of experience behind him, could do it with his voice. Powell describes how he was shown by a man of a jungle tribe how to make a device that could be used to call either tiger or panther. He improved on it and found it indispensable when summoning a panther, as the only effective method of imitating their distinctive call, a sound like the double stroke of a man sawing a heavy plank. He is discreetly silent in his book as to any details of the device. On further enquiry he explains that he has two reasons for his reticence. The rather obvious one is that he does not want the idea to be exploited by the unscrupulous; but there was also the element of personal risk. He did at first pass on the idea to several friends, but after 'two or three had been chewed up', not by tigers but by panthers, he thought it wiser to keep the secret to himself. The point is that the call has to be made from ground level. A tiger calling for a mate does not sit up a tree, and if the call comes from a machan the animal answering it will detect the trick before he is within shooting distance. If he accepts the call as genuine he does not necessarily answer and may appear suddenly and from any direction. 'One meets one's quarry on the level, a few yards away in dense cover.' An animal, excited at the prospect of meeting a mate, that finds it has been the victim of a stupid practical joke is in no mood to be trifled with. Swift and decisive action is the order of the day.

# 8. Panthers and Man-eaters

*Unsuspecting villager*

The leopard, or panther, is found over the length and breadth of the Indian peninsula. It is at home in widely differing surroundings, so it is not surprising that it varies widely in size and colouring, so much so that the theory has from time to time been put forward, only to be exploded, that there are two completely different animals, to which the name of panther and leopard should respectively be given. There is, in fact, only one species; the name is a matter of personal preference. The snow leopard of the Himalayas is a separate beast and is always so called, but for the animal over the rest of India the word panther seems to trip more readily off the tongue, and it is by that name that it will be called in this book.

Dunbar Brander lists its diet as consisting of sows, small pigs, cattle, calves, donkeys, ponies, young buffaloes, goats, sheep, dogs, jackals, blackbuck, chinkara, four-horned antelope, barking deer, mouse deer, monkeys, hares, peafowl, jungle fowl, porcupines and even crabs, snakes and lizards. Its size varies with its diet. A small animal hanging round the outskirts of a village may weigh as little as 50 lb, the average is rather more than double that figure, while a gol bagh (spotted tiger), living in jungles where it has to deal with the larger deer, may run up to as much as 160 lb; its method of killing and eating its prey resembling those of a tiger.

The sportsman setting out to shoot a panther proceeded with just as much caution as if he were after a tiger, for the risks were pretty much the same. If you were mauled by a tiger that was likely to be the end of you; with a panther you had a sporting chance but would carry the scars for the rest of your life.

Stuart Baker, going to the rescue of a servant attacked by a panther, was himself so badly mauled that his arm was left hanging by a strip of flesh. His wife cut it off with the carving knife. He survived not only to write his remarkable bird books but to go on shooting with one arm.

The panther is so small that it can take advantage of the least scrap of cover, and its behaviour is completely unpredictable, varying from cowardice to foolhardy determination. The maternal instinct is strongly developed and Anderson has a story of a female panther whose cubs were wantonly butchered by a woodcutter. She became an inveterate man-killer, killer not eater, wreaking her vengeance on any luckless human being when she thought she could get away with it.

The panther is more intelligent than the tiger and more cunning, and when these qualities are sharpened by familiarity with the ways of man, gained from living on the outskirts of a village or military station, your sophisticated panther presents a challenge to even the most experienced sportsman.

Panthers are very partial to dogs, and many men, although alive to the risk, have lost favourite terriers or spaniels. There is even a story of one being taken from the end of its master's camp bed as both lay asleep in the open.

The panther is universally detested, and when he is on the move in the jungle, no doubt to his intense annoyance, not only the deer and the monkeys give the alarm but 'plovers, peafowl, crows and babblers follow him along the treetops, cawing and chattering, while even squirrels and tree shrews will chirrup and demonstrate'.

There is a sinister look about him as though he is 'made of velvet, rubber and steel springs, supple as a snake and nearly as wicked looking'. But he is a thing of beauty in his winter coat, 'marked over with black rosettes as if the five fingers of the hand had been bunched up, dipped in soot and impressed on the yellow skin'.

In *Hunter's Moon* Handley was sitting up for a panther.

> 'I rose almost imperceptibly on one elbow and faced a full grown panther—crouched in the moonlight within twenty yards of the kill; ready to spring.
>
> 'Though I hang on with senile fingers to this travesty men call modern life for a full hundred years I shall never forget the beauty of that crouching figure. Drenched in the ghost light, it crouched, the embodiment of benevolent grace. Poised for its fatal spring, every muscle rippled beneath the beautiful silver body. The eyes flashed emerald, and the whole figure seemed as though poured from some gigantic ladle of molten silver.'

Living more in the open their eyesight was even keener than that of the tiger.

> 'He approached with a movement so slow as to be imperceptible to the eye, and he must have taken fully half an hour to reach the rock below which I had tied the goat. At one time I blinked an eye, and the faraway look that is so characteristic of the great cats changed at once into an intense frown, and a couple of minutes must have passed before I saw the scrutiny relax.'

It was difficult to drive a panther because of the ease with which he managed to conceal himself and his habit of breaking back through the beaters. Sitting up was the more general method of shooting them. In the jungle, the procedure was the same as for a tiger; in the scrub-covered rocky country that they favoured, the plan was to sit behind a rocky outcrop, or behind a screen of thorn bush or leaves. One writer explains that the only equipment needed was a hatchet, to cut the branches; a church hassock, to sit on; a trowel, to dig a pit for the feet and a square of felt to deaden the noise made if you fidgetted while you were waiting. It all sounds too easy, but in fact very great skill and experience were needed in selecting the actual site for the hide and for tying the kill. In that lay more than half the battle. The same writer admits that when young and full of enthusiasm he tied up baits for an entire year and must have sat over them nearly a hundred times before he secured his first panther.

The approach to shooting a tiger or panther so far has been from the point of view of an ordinary sportsman, with no great experience to guide him, trying to outwit an animal with no direct personal contact with man; one who might have killed the odd village buffalo or cow, but in the main lived on food provided by nature; one who had not been shot at, or at any rate had not been wounded. Amateur played amateur, and if the animal got away no great harm had been done.

Complications set in if you shot at and wounded a tiger and it got away. It goes without saying that it became your personal responsibility to follow it and deal with it. Following a wounded tiger is probably the most dangerous game on earth if only because of the animal's remarkable vitality.

Dunbar Brander had a remarkable escape.

> 'A cat has nine lives and the tiger is the largest and strongest cat in the world. I was once nearly killed by assuming that a tiger which was bleeding in the face from the spot at which I had aimed was dead. It lay there apparently dead. It had previously been wounded and had already given me two charges and a lot of trouble. Thankful that this was now all over, I stepped forward without even reloading the empty barrel when it suddenly sprang up with a roar and rushed at me. I was lucky enough to get it in the nostrils and did kill it this time, but its dead body in turning over struck me in the chest and in turn laid me out for some minutes.'

A well-trained elephant was invaluable when following up a wounded tiger, but few men had them and the rule then was to proceed with the greatest caution. To the experienced, the blood trail might reveal the nature and severity of the wound, enabling one to deduce his moves and where he might be lying up. The cries of jungle animals and birds might betray his whereabouts.

The man who came to shoot for sport only might find, on reaching his block, that a confirmed cattle killer or man-eater with a price on its head was on the rampage. He would not refuse to tackle it, but he entered the professional league with his eyes open. He would be luck to succeed, and if he shot and missed the beast would become more cunning, more cautious and more determined than ever to wreak its vengeance on the human race. Corbett, when asked to take on a man-eater, always stipulated that any enthusiastic amateur who might be trying to deal with it, should clear out and leave the field to him.

Tigers and panthers became man-eaters for all sorts of reasons, but it could happen that the first step was taken when indiscriminate slaughter of the tiger's food, by villagers trying to protect their crops, upset the balance of nature. He then started to take regular toll of domestic cattle. The villagers would then take the law into their own hands and have a go with some antiquated musket, licensed to them for crop protection, and more often than not they would only wound the marauder. If the result was permanent damage to the jaws or a limb that made it difficult for the animal to kill its natural food, then it would not be long before it turned to eating man.

When threatened by a confirmed man-eater, the villagers were helpless, though there are stories of incredible bravery in the face of danger. Anderson tells of a father who volunteered to be sat over as a bait, if by doing so he could avenge the death of his daughter.

Jim Corbett in *The Temple Tiger* writes:

> 'Those who have never lived in an area in which a man-eating tiger is operating may be inclined to think that there is nothing courageous in a mother going out to look for her son, in two boys grazing cattle, or in a party of men going out to look for a missing boy. But to one who has lived in such an area the entry of the mother into a dense patch of jungle in which she knew there was an angry tiger; the two small boys sitting close together for protection; and the party of men following on the blood trail left by a man-eater, were acts calling for a measure of courage that merited the greatest admiration.'

It was bad enough if the man-eater ranged over a wide area; if he concentrated his attacks, community life was paralysed and complete villages might be abandoned. The situation then became urgent and formidable in its difficulty. There were no full-time game wardens so the task had to be undertaken by a Corbett or an Anderson, a forest officer, or the deputy commissioner of the district.

To give some idea of the extent of the menace, Corbett quotes the case of a man-eater which arrived in the Kumaon from Nepal with a reputed 200 victims to his name, and over the next four years killed a further 234 before he was shot—a man or a woman every week. And at different times, two panthers between them killed 525 people. As all the time attempts were being made to shoot these pests, it is clear just how hard it was to deal with a man-eater.

The crux of the matter was that you were trying to bring to very close quarters, for you could not afford to miss, an animal whose natural caution and cunning were enhanced by bitter experience; and in conditions in which the role of hunter and hunted might dramatically be reversed. If you were on the trail of a man-eater every bush, tree and rock, every dip in the ground along the path, had to be approached with caution on the assumption that behind it the animal might be sitting up for you. Corbett, perhaps through long experience, says that he developed a sixth sense that time and again warned him of impending danger.

The essential preliminary was a careful study of the animal's history. The man-eater, just as much as the man setting out to shoot him, was an individual and developed a pattern of behaviour all its own. A very high standard of jungle craft was called for; the ability to interpret the calls of the animal itself, and of other jungle animals who were warning you of its whereabouts, to distinguish its tracks from those of others and to read from them where it had come from and where, probably, it was going. And you might have to do all this for yourself. On balance you were better off moving alone, you then had only your own safety to think of. Paradoxically you did not always get the help you might expect from the local inhabitants. Superstition sometimes came into it. The spirit of the last departed, whose death you were out to avenge, was reputed to sit on the head of the tiger and guide it to its next victim. When men believed that, they were reluctant to become implicated.

It was seldom possible to set up a beat for a man-eater as might be done for an ordinary tiger; he would be too cunning and would break back, and anyway the lives of the beaters could not be put at risk. Again, a man-eater was cautious about returning to a kill, particularly if his highly developed suspicions had been aroused; and when a man had been killed there was seldom enough left of the remains to make it worth while doing so.

The movements of an animal on the prowl in a given area could be forecast to some extent and a machan put up over a path he was in the habit of using, but on the whole more positive action was called for. When a man-eater had been located time was all important. If not shot he might kill again or, even worse, vanish only to reappear 35 or 40 miles away when all the preliminary work in the way of reconnaissance would have to be done afresh. This was when things became really tough. There were two alternatives, each fraught with danger. The first was to follow up and stalk him, accepting the risk that he might be stalking you; the other was to call him up.

There are plenty of stories about man-eaters, and during the last thirty years both Jim Corbett and Kenneth Anderson have written of their experiences. Their books are available in most county libraries. Apart from their merit as records of what these men did, you may think as you finish a story that the point that really matters has not been made. The terrifying personal risks, accepted in full knowledge of what they are taking on, are invariably written down. They were just part of what they set out to do. And for what reward? Perhaps a paltry Rs125—say £15—if government had put a

*The Man-eater's Victim*

price on a man-eater's head: but neither man ever bothered to claim the money. Enough for them was the gratitude of a handful of ignorant villagers whose dead they had avenged, who had been freed from the haunting possibility of meeting a grisly end. Gratitude was all that mattered.

It is a little invidious to pick out any of these stories for special mention, but it is proposed to take a brief look at Corbett's story, *The Thak Man-eater*. It covers pretty well every aspect of what was involved, and the cliff-hanging suspense of the final half-hour is such that no writer would ever have the temerity to expect his readers to credit it if presented as a piece of fiction.

Early one September Corbett received the news that a twelve-year-old girl had been killed in an area marked by the forest department for extensive tree felling, due to start in November. Unless the man-eater was shot before then there was the fear that the contractors would be unable to persuade the woodcutters to remain at work.

Making a detour to avoid a heavily malarious area involved a march of 150 miles, and while Corbett was making his preparations an old woman was killed in the next village. The matter had now become serious, and he was joined by the deputy commissioner of the district. The two men arrived in the area towards the end of October and at once found the tracks of a tigress thought to be responsible. An examination of the pug marks showed her to be an average sized animal in the prime of life. Buffaloes were tied up without success, then on the 27th a man was killed. They found his loincloth and cap, and decided to try to stalk the tigress and shoot her on the kill. In two hours they covered half a mile. They surprised her behind a rock but she saw them first and got away. Then they found the body and decided to sit up, and Corbett had the unsavoury task of moving the remains a few feet to give a better chance of a shot. She did not return, though she followed the rest of the party as they went back to the village in the hope of picking up another victim.

Two nights later a bullock was killed, and with the tigress calling in the valley below, a rough machan was put up, no more than a few strands of rope tied between two branches.

> 'I took my seat on what, during the next fourteen hours, proved to be the most uncomfortable as well as the most dangerous machan I have ever sat on. The tree was leaning away from the hill, and from the three uneven strands of rope I was sitting on there was a drop of over a hundred feet into the ravine below.'

But it was a blank night and next day he was left alone as the deputy commissioner had pressing duties elsewhere. On November 7th Corbett himself returned home, having been away nearly a month. On the 12th another man was killed, and by doing forced marches he was back in the area soon after sunrise on the 24th. Thousands of woodcutters were arriving but every man, woman and child had left the village where the man had been killed. Corbett visited the scene. Everywhere in the dust were pug marks, and the open doorways were a menace, as in any one of them the tigress might have been lurking. On the way down, at a spring where he had drunk on the way up, he found her footmarks superimposed on his own. She had been following him.

When he left home he had promised his sister that he would return at the end of the month, and give up shooting man-eaters: for good. So he had six days and nights left. On November 27th he sat up, and when at sunset a cold wind sprang up and he was trying to pull a coat over his shoulders, the ropes on one side of the machan slipped rendering his seat 'very uncomfortable'. An hour later a storm blew up and wet him to the skin. On the 29th a deputation visited him to say that if, as they had heard, he proposed to leave on the 30th, the entire army of woodcutters would march out with him. That night he sat up again but the tigress visited the labour camps, and when the men shouted to drive her away she became infuriated and demonstrated till she cowed them into silence.

On November 30th, his last day, he tried to tempt her with a couple of goats. He sat over them till four o'clock when the sun set behind the hills and the wind became unbearably cold. It brought on an attack of ague and he realised that if the tigress came he would be unable to hit her. He was the victim of depression following failure, for he had been on the heels of the man-eater from October 23rd to November 7th, and again from November 24th to 30th.

> 'It is only those of you who have walked in fear of having the teeth of a tiger meet in your throat who will have any idea of the effect on the nerves of days and weeks of such anticipation.'

The only thing to do was to begin the weary trek back to camp, but when he met the men who were waiting for him they told him they had heard the tigress calling from some distance away. Suddenly he heard the call across a valley to his left. The sun was casting a red glow on the peaks, but he had half an hour's daylight in hand, long enough for the tigress to cross the wooded, rock strewn valley: if she wanted to. He decided to call her up. It was a desperate expedient; if she came and he shot her, all would be well. If not, then some one of the party would not survive the two miles back to camp through heavy jungle. He waited till she called again then, 'cupping my hands round my mouth and filling my lungs to their utmost limit', he sent an answering call. For several minutes call answered call. She was on her way.

Pressing down the path in search of a place where he could meet her he found a large rock. On it was a narrow ledge on which he could just sit, but to secure a hold he must extend his left hand over the rounded top of the rock, and by extending his right leg to its full extent he could just touch the ground with his toes. The heavy rifle, resting on the naked rock, would be held in his right hand only. It would be pointing along the path in which there was a slight hump, and it was his intention to fire at the tigress's face as she came into view, twenty feet away. The tigress had located the call but misjudged the distance so came at a slightly different angle from that he had expected. She was working herself into a perfect fury and in less than a minute it would be too dark to shoot. Something had to be done, and done quickly. He called again, and so did the tigress. She changed direction slightly and

> 'the full blast of her deep-throated call struck me in the face and would have carried the hat off my head if I had been wearing one.'

By great and unexpected good luck she appeared at the exact spot at which his rifle was pointing. The first bullet caught her under the right eye, the second, fired more by accident than intent, in the throat. The recoil from the first barrel loosened his hold on the rock, the second took him in the jaw and sent him head over heels on top of the men crouching under the rock below him. They caught him as he fell and saved him from injury, and the rifle from being broken.

The rest of the story is something of an anti-climax. Men swarming in by the hundred to see the body; skinning it in the dark with a pen knife; and the discovery of wounds in both shoulders, inflicted by buckshot, that had gone septic and probably turned her into a man-eater.

> 'I bathed and dressed and though my face was swollen and painful and I had twenty miles of rough going before me I left walking on air, while thousands of men in and around the valley were peacefully sleeping.'

# 9. Buffalo, Bison and Others

*Sambhur*

Tiger and panther take pride of place in most game books because they were plentiful and because of the element of personal danger that might be involved if things went wrong when you set out to shoot them. There were four other animals of the jungle that were potentially dangerous; elephant, rhinoceros, bison and buffalo. The first two have been dealt with in Chapter 3, covering the days when they might be shot by the unprivileged sportsman, and little more need now be said about them.

There were a few elephants in both the United and Central Provinces; they were more numerous in Assam, Nepal and the jungles of the south-west, notably in Mysore, where they were the preserve of the maharajah. Except for the occasional rogue they were never shot.

The rhinoceros survived in small numbers in Burma, and in India in the Nepal Terai where only very important persons and their staffs were invited by the maharajah to shoot them. There is a reference to this in Chapter 17 in connection with the visit of the then Prince of Wales to India in the cold weather of 1921–2.

In the game book of that tour it is recorded that the Prince and his staff shot 30 tigers, 6 panthers, 3 elephants and 10 rhinoceros.

One member of the staff, an equerry more adventurous than his fellows, went after a bison for two days in Burma and shot it, but there is no mention of the buffalo. The fact is that these two were no game for those who shot only from a machan or the back of an elephant. Their pursuit entailed an early start through soaking grass, considerable hardship and endurance, much patience and sustained interest and, in the case of the buffalo, the possibility of an encounter with a remorseless enemy armed with an enormous pair of sharp horns.

The bison, to give it the name by which it was generally and mistakenly known, does not belong to the bison family. Its correct name is gaur and it is a species of wild ox. They were found in India in the Central Provinces and to the south, and also in Assam and Burma. They are hill animals and only come down to the lower levels in search of water during the hot weather. The bull bison is an immense black animal, standing perhaps 5 ft 6 in at the shoulder and weighing three quarters of a ton. The legs and feet are small considering the weight they have to carry. Both sexes carry horns, and the best heads were found in Burma and south India.

Living mainly in thick jungle, their eyesight is poor and like most noisy animals their hearing far from acute, but they have a highly developed sense of smell, and with the wind in the right direction, can detect presence of man from as far as 400 yards away. Their only enemies are man and the tiger. The latter might kill a calf but would be quite incapable of breaking the neck of a full grown animal. A pair of tigers might take on a bison but they would deal with it by first biting through the hock and hamstringing it. Bison seemed to have an instinctive fear of man, not really justified by any inherited threat of danger, as they were seldom shot even by poachers among the aboriginal tribes. Nevertheless, once alarmed they cover immense distances at not much more than a fast walk, but they can keep it up indefinitely over the most impossible country.

A solitary animal was likely to be a bull, but when encountering a herd a novice might have trouble in distinguishing between the sexes when, as often happened, the body was only partially visible in thick jungle. A shooting permit might impose quite a heavy fine for shooting a cow, if only to encourage the inexperienced to make a study beforehand of the difference in the formation of the horns which, failing an all-over view, was the only certain way of distinguishing them.

Even when wounded, the bison was not a wilfully vicious animal. Any reputation he had for being so was due to his own behaviour, enlarged on through ignorance by the inexperienced. When fired at

*Bull Bison*

he would be likely to whip round, trying blindly to identify his aggressor. The latter thinking he was about to be charged promptly fired into the bison's chest, the least vulnerable part of his body. An animal's instinct when struck is to charge in the direction in which it is facing. He 'blunders wildly forward, and the young hunter returns with yet another tale of a charging bison, when as a matter of fact no such intention ever entered its mind.'

The buffalo resembles the bison in that both are large heavy animals with horns. He is only slightly the larger but his horns are magnificent; in the record specimen a single horn measured just over 77 inches. He is the same animal as the domestic beast, but perhaps because he enjoys, from birth, a plentiful supply of the food nature intended for him, he is much larger. He has the same liking for water and for wallowing and is found in low-lying grassy plains, affording plenty of shade. On the outskirts of civilisation a wild bull might assume mastery of a village herd and, if excessively amorous and possessive, he might even prevent the rightful owners from approaching it. Buffaloes could also do considerable damage to crops, and if they failed to drive them off the villagers might resort to shooting them with guns or poisoned arrows. Even when not wounded the buffalo was potentially extremely dangerous.

The procedure for tracking both bison and buffalo was very much the same. Against these massive, thick-skinned animals the only safe weapon was a heavy rifle, weighing as much as 12 lb and firing a solid bullet, and however hot, difficult and long the trail, you carried it yourself in a constant state of readiness. You were completely in the hands of your trackers. Powell describes the attractions of watching them at work.

> 'The trackers fanned out until with a click of the tongue and a broad smile one of them called us over to where he had found unmistakable signs. The first rays of the sun began lighting up the treetops and we found ourselves submerged in a sea of grass. Bending down from time to time they separated the tangled grass and examined the tracks to make sure they had not lost the trail in the mass of tracks crossing and re-crossing. Except for their loin-cloths they were stark naked and they were shivering from the icy cold dewdrops sparkling on their bare bodies. It was my duty to look ahead and to the flanks, but during a check it was a pleasure to watch them almost sniffing out the scent, discovering the minutest clues. A nibbled blade of grass, a bit of bark rubbed off a tree or creeper by the big horns passing, an upturned pebble, a twig snapped underfoot, a leaf dangling from a broken stem.'

The most difficult part of the trail was at the beginning when a maze of tracks criss-crossed in a small area, and it seemed little short of a miracle that your trackers were able to pick out one and follow it by signs that were not even visible to your inexperienced eye. Once a single bull had been identified the hunt would begin in earnest; you were on the trail of the animal you eventually hoped to shoot. He might go on for hours and there would be checks from time to time where the beast had paused to graze, an occasional cast around for fresh traces till the moment when unmistakable signs showed that at last you were closing up on him. A pile of fresh, steaming dung reminded you that your absorption in the skill of your trackers must not blind you to your own responsibility: to be alert, to watch ahead, with your rifle ready to take the fleeting chance that might be offered. Should you fail in your duty, there would be a crash and your quarry would be gone before you could fire. In his *Shikar Notes for Novices*, Best underlines the sportsman's responsibility:

> 'He had probably been quietly watching you for the last half minute and offering a splendid shot. The trackers' quiet contempt at your ignorance of their art will, after this incident, be replaced by annoyance and disgust at your incompetence, and if the incident is repeated, by suspicions of your courage.'

You would then be wise to pause to let the animal quieten down, in the hope that he would decide that this was no more than a chance encounter. The trail would be taken up again till at last a touch on the arm and a pointing hand

> 'a hundred yards away stands a magnificent animal with a pair of horns such as you never hoped to see in your wildest dreams; head up half facing you, and stamping his forefeet; it is clear he resents this intrusion and means to look into it. If your trackers now vanish behind substantial trees you cannot blame them, as you are now up against one of the finest, and one of the most active, vicious and relentless beasts of the forest.'

It will take both barrels and perhaps several more shots from your spare magazine rifle before he falls.

> '. . . your heart swells with joy and pride at securing a good specimen of the finest trophy in India, feelings soon to be replaced by an uncomfortable one of shame and sorrow at destroying so splendid and gallant life.'

## THE BEAR

The bear of the jungle is the sloth bear. Scientific evidence establishes him as a separate genus and fossilised remains prove that he has existed in India from the very earliest years. The picture of him in *The Jungle Book* is a little misleading: Baloo, the sleepy brown bear, infinitely wise and gentle, who taught Mowgli the law of the jungle, who came and went as he pleased because he only ate roots and nuts and wild honey. True enough of his relations with the other animals, for they had nothing to fear from him, nor he from them. But because of his completely unpredictable character, there was none more dreaded by the villagers. Woe to the man who stumbled unawares upon a bear. The lacerated faces to be met in any locality where bears were numerous, testified to the damage he could do.

With all respect to Kipling, he is not brown but black; a large shaggy animal, weighing as much as 350 lb, with a white horseshoe on his chest, a whitish, mangy looking face, hairless rims to his wicked little eyes and large dirty grey protruding lips and snout. But the business end of the bear lies in his claws, white and ruthlessly sharp and some four inches long. Designed by nature for digging and for climbing trees, they make short work of a man's face and scalp. He is immensely powerful and possessed of great vitality.

The maternal instinct is very strong and a she-bear disturbed with cubs is likely to make an unprovoked attack. A bear cub up to the size of a small terrier may be carried pick-a-back to and from feeding grounds, retaining its seat even when its mother is travelling full tilt over very rough ground. Like the bison, a noisy animal living in dense jungle, the bear's hearing and sight are poor, and this accounts for his erratically dangerous behaviour. He would not hear the approach of the man who stumbled across him, then, surprised at short range by a figure he could not identify, he would charge, inflict two or three scalping wounds with those terrible claws and disappear into the jungle. His sense of smell is something of a paradox. In the detection of grubs and roots for food it is undoubtedly acute, but you might come down wind on a bear which had received no warning of your arrival. Dunbar Brander suggests that his sense of smell is developed to meet the peculiar needs of his daily life, and that he is in fact 'short scented'.

His diet is very varied; fruit, tubers, insects, grubs and honey, and in search of the quantity needed to sustain an animal of his size, he has to travel great distances and know through the seasons of the year where he can find his food. He has to dig, and in dealing with a white ants' nest he will first demolish the base till he comes to the core. The fine dust dispelled by blowing, he then sucks the entire contents of the nest into his mouth. He has to be able to climb, and not only in search of fruit. He may have taught Mowgli 'how to speak politely to the wild bees when he came upon a hive of them fifty feet above the ground', but when foraging for himself he does not stand on ceremony. He knocks the comb bodily to the ground and deals with it later at his leisure.

Dunbar Brander describes how they forage for insects under stones:

> 'On one occasion while sitting on the banks of a jungle stream in Chanda I witnessed this performance. It was about ten o'clock and a beautiful moonlight night. My attention was first of all drawn by a most singular bubbling, squealing and squeaking, accompanied by a noise that sounded like a cart being driven over stones. The noise gradually approached and presently two bears fed right past me. The noise like the cart was caused by the clattering of the displaced stones, and the bubbling and squeaking was a conversation in bear language, probably expressing their pleasure and the extent of their luck as each stone was turned. I have never heard such an extraordinary mixture of sounds, or such a sustained conversation expressed by any animal.'

In parts of the Central Provinces a reward of five rupees was paid for shooting a bear, prompted by the need to keep the numbers down to reasonable proportions in areas where villagers and forest workers going about their lawful occasions might suffer from their attacks. The reward was not large enough to appeal to the sportsman on leave in search of other game, nor was it an inducement to the village shikari to risk a mauling in the pursuit on foot of an animal he so rightly dreaded. The skin of a bear made a fine rug, but they were mostly shot on chance encounters, or if they came out in a beat arranged for a tiger. Questing in the dawn light in the spring, when the mohwa flowers with their luscious juice carpet the ground under the trees you might come across a bear guzzling a favourite delicacy. But before firing it was as well to be sure that you had not drawn a bead on some village beldam, sent out to gather a sackful of the raw material from which would be distilled a potent brand of local spirit.

The bear, if only wounded, will set up a hideous clamour of protest, and if in company with other bears at once assume that his neighbour is the guilty party; and attack him accordingly. Dunbar Brander has a story of shooting a single bear that emerged in a beat, not knowing that it was not alone. When he shot it, it at once turned and savaged the bear behind it, and in a matter of seconds, to the accompaniment of an appalling noise, a seething mass of four bears, locked in deadly combat, rolled down into the nullah.

It goes without saying that when shooting a bear on foot, and particularly if the animal had been wounded, it was wise to retain the tactical advantage by keeping above your quarry.

## THE DEER

There are four varieties of deer in the jungle; the sambhur, the swamp deer or barasingh, the cheetal or spotted deer, and the barking deer. They are listed in order of their size, the difficulty of shooting them, and the significance of their horns as trophies. They might all be shot for meat, the barking deer being seldom shot for any other reason. In general only stags were shot, though if herds became large enough to present a real nuisance to crops, a specified number of hinds might be included in a permit.

The Monarch of the Glen is the sambhur. His horns may lack the spread of the barasingh or the graceful symmetry of the cheetal, but they make up for it in size and weight, and the rough corrugations of the horns of a mature stag give a great impression of rugged strength. The brow tine comes out at an acute angle, then the main beam divides, high up, into two branches which conform to no set pattern;

they may be equal, or the inner or outer may be the longer. A 40-inch head was considered good. The coat is coarse and shaggy, the colour, dark brown. The height of an average stag is 55 inches at the shoulder and the weight 610 lb. He appears in the sketch at the head of this chapter.

The horns are shed in the early spring. They are in velvet throughout the rainy season and are clear by mid November in time for the rut which takes place early in December. The fact that the sambhur lives in thick jungle rules out the collection of large herds, and master stags fight for territory which carry with it the favours of the hinds that live there. But fight they do, and with great determination, to assert their rights within their chosen valley.

Their staple diet is grass but they browse extensively, eating a variety of leaves and fruit and may also do damage to crops on the edge of the jungle. Their habits are largely nocturnal, they lie up early in the day and do not emerge until late afternoon. The sambhur is hunted by the tiger and by wild dogs, and also by man, and as he is not a prolific breeder, has developed protective faculties and instincts (particularly the senses of scent and hearing) to a degree far beyond those of any other deer or antelope. Given reasonable conditions of locality and season, you should within a span of fourteen days, be able to shoot a warrantable specimen of any selected species: it might be months before you secured a good sambhur stag. The stalk was the accepted method of setting about it.

For the best chance of success you must discover a likely site, a salt lick or the fruit trees of a deserted village, and be in the locality by dawn or mid-afternoon. The approach had to be up-wind and the final stage consisted of moving with the utmost caution, literally step by step, in the hope that you would locate a stag, possibly by its peculiar acrid smell, before he became aware of the danger and went crashing off into the jungle. An alternative method was to beat and, provided this was not held to include the indiscriminate sweep of a whole hillside, it was a form of sport which called for much skill and knowledge of the animal's habit and of the terrain. The crux of the matter was that the instinct of self-preservation was so highly developed. Tiger, panther or bear might be pushed along in a beat with a reasonable degree of firmness. A sambhur had to be coaxed. Noise or undue haste inevitably spelt failure.

The swamp deer or barasingh (twelve pointer) is a handsome beast with a brown coat, and of all the Indian deer it most closely resembles the European species. The horns are not so massive or large as the sambhur, 35 inches was considered a good head, but they spread outwards from the brow tine and, after growing vertically, curve abruptly forward when the first tine appears. Dunbar Brander considered it to be one of the most beautiful horns in the world. He gives the height of a stag at 54 inches and the weight at 370 lb.

When the rutting season begins in December, they fight savagely for their rights over a collection of hinds, usually much larger than they can in fact look after, and they frequently have to interrupt the business in hand to chase away smaller stags, too young to have collected a harem of their own. When the rut is over the big master stags form small herds of companions of their own weight; membership being as highly selective as that of the most exclusive club. Stags found with the general herds are not then really worth shooting.

> 'The roaring of the stags is a sound which cannot be compared with that of any other wild animal in India . . . It begins with a loud and penetrating "ring-hon ring-hon", which is repeated in gradually decreasing volume as the air in the lungs becomes exhausted: but in addition to this call there is an accompanying drone which is kept going all the time the call is being repeated. No one who hears this call for the first time can help being struck by the strangeness of the sound, and few will escape without a feeling of undefined weirdness engendered in his being. Even amongst those who are accustomed to the sound, conversation at the camp fire usually ceases until the call has ended.'

In the United Provinces the swamp deer lived up to its name by frequenting areas where water was plentiful. In the Central Provinces, where this type of country was very rare, they preferred large open plains with plenty of grass for grazing. Living in the open their eyesight is better than that of the sambhur, and they have an acute sense of smell but the general sense of self-preservation is not so highly developed.

The barasingh was the natural prey of tiger, panther and wild dog and suffered much at the hands of village poachers, armed with weapons licensed for crop protection, though this particular species did little or no damage to cultivation. The accepted method of shooting was the stalk, with the complication that the height of the surrounding grass might balk your shot when at last you had approached to within firing distance. You had also to remember that if you were looking for a really fine head the smaller and more secluded patches of grass were the places in which to look.

A lightweight compared with the sambhur and barasingh, the cheetal has a grace all of its own, the head of the stag adorned by a pair of lyre-shaped horns of perfect symmetry. A head of 35 inches was considered good: a stag might stand 36 inches at the shoulder and weigh just under 200 lb.

The rut is in March and the stags fight for mastery over the herd of hinds they collect. The warning cry is a shrill whistle. They are thirsty animals, requiring a plentiful water supply and open gladed forests. They are comparatively tolerant of the presence of man and move down at night to feed on village crops. They were shot by stalking, which required a careful approach; the most successful method being to visit at dawn the paths they used moving back to the forests from the cultivated areas.

The kakar or barking deer is a small animal, the buck standing 24 inches at the shoulder and weighing no more than 40 lb. The horns over the curves may be 6 inches long. They are widely distributed over India, living in the Himalayas up to a height of 6,000 feet. The loud staccato bark from which they get their name is one of the most familiar sounds of the jungle for they are always the first to give the alarm if tiger or panther is on the move, but unless you set out to look you would seldom see one. They live in pairs in shady bamboo-clad ravines and will not move far afield even in search of food. They are dainty feeders and their flesh is the most tasty of all deer, but that was seldom held to be a reason for shooting them. If you had an evening to spare and were interested in the ways of animals you would be well repaid by a visit towards dusk to some shady ravine where you might watch them feeding.

## THE ANTELOPES

There were three antelopes the sportsman might meet: the chinkara or Indian gazelle, the nilgai or blue bull and the blackbuck. They might be found in open jungle where there were large open expanses of grass, but they were really animals of the plains.

The habitat of the chinkara was open scrub jungle and among low foothills. His protective colouring was good and it was hard to pick him out. He relied on his speed for safety but was preyed on by hyenas, wild dogs, jackals and even eagles. Rather than shoot, it was more rewarding to watch him through glasses as he picked his dainty way through the bushes, feeding as he went.

The nilgai was an ungainly animal the size of a country pony. He took his name from his resemblance to the domestic cow, and was accordingly held in reverence by Hindus. He earned the ignoble distinction of carrying the poorest trophy of any animal of his size.

In herds of a dozen or more he might do great damage to crops, and this was the only real reason for shooting him.

The blackbuck is another animal altogether. A good buck might stand 32 inches at the shoulder and weigh 90 lb. and for his size he carries the finest head of any antelope in the world. The horn is a long screw spiral, the record 30 inches, though of more recent times anything from 22 to 25 inches was considered good. He is probably also the fastest animal in the world over a distance, and can keep up a speed of 40 m.p.h. indefinitely.

> 'I believe that if it were possible to enter a herd of black buck for the Derby and their pace to be regulated by the slowest animal they would come in a solid mob well in front of the horses and, given anything in the way of jumps or uneven ground, the relative speed of buck and horse would be further accentuated.'

He was common over the open plains of north-west India where there was no jungle in the accepted sense of the word, and did much damage to crops. He was easy to pick up but he had better eyes than you had and was invariably surrounded by his 'sentinel does, noses thrust out, ears hingeing to and fro', alert to the first scent of danger. If you got within range it was not always easy to find a position from which to shoot, and a writer to *The Field* describes how patient you had to be.

> 'I had done fairly well, when one day I spotted afar off a buck as black as your hat and with, I am convinced, twenty four inch horns. It was too late to do anything that day but next day I was out after him with never a sight. Daylight on the third day, the last day of my leave, found me out again and after two hours search I found him on utterly impossible ground, a wide plain sparsely dotted with clumps of bush; wind wrong, sun wrong, everything was wrong.
>
> 'I came to the conclusion that the only thing to do was to drive him, if I could, on to the ground which would give me a better chance to approach. He had left the herd so I thought it might be done, and then began a most absurd game into which the buck seemed to enter with zest, as though he knew all about it. Do what I could, I could not get him to do what I wanted; if I stopped, he stopped, if I went on, he went on, but never in the direction I wanted him to, and always was well beyond the dead sure range outside which I never shot.

'After some hours of this game he topped a rise and disappeared, but on to some ground where I knew there was a depression between two ridges where a dry nullah ran through it. If he stopped in the hollow and I could get round so as to approach him over the far ridge, up wind, I ought to get him. This meant a big chukkar round and as I crossed the nullah I debated whether I would crawl up it and try to get him that way but decided not to, for if he had already crossed the nullah the wind would still be wrong.

'So I kept on round, and after about an hour I, in my turn, topped the opposite ridge, now moving directly up wind, after having completely lost sight of the buck for over an hour. And there he was, not twenty yards away, alternately grazing and looking up in the direction from which he obviously expected me. The rest was butchery. I crawled over the ridge on my belly and looked through a bush.

'I had only to raise the rifle and he was done, when a revulsion of feeling came over me. Why should I kill him? I had won hands down and could exercise my prerogative of mercy, so I stood up and took my hat off to him. For one minute he stood looking at me with his off fore hoof well off the ground, then he was gone and I saw him in the flesh no more. On the wall of my room hang two shields, each carrying a head of one of those two twenty-one inch buck I had shot on that trip. And in the middle, between them hangs an empty shield. On it I often see in imagination the head of the finest black buck I ever shot.'

There was one animal, a sheep, that under different names was found on both plain and hill: the oorial of the Salt Range, the shapoo of the Indus valley in Ladakh and Baltistan. The shapoo was always overshadowed by his larger cousins—a good oorial head was a trophy anyone could be proud of. And you shot him on ten days' leave in the cold weather, without all the trouble and expense of crossing the Himalayas.

In *Stalks in the Himalayas,* Stebbing describes the Salt Range, the inhospitable tract of low hills along the left bank of the Indus, south of the Grand Trunk Road from Rawalpindi to Peshawar.

'In the lower portions of the Salt Range and in the stony hills of the Punjab the temperature runs up in the summer months to a fierce, furnace heat, and the hot winds blow with a persistent and burning intensity that has to be experienced to be believed . . . Yet the country has a peculiar fascination, wild, barren rock and desert, the hills shapes cut into a thousand shapes sharp and hard as the cruel blue of the sky above them, while their sides take on in the evening a fascinating medley of crude colouring, browns and reds and yellows.'

The writer does not exaggerate, but in fact no one in his senses went there in summer. He would not live to tell the tale. Only for a few weeks on either side of the New Year was the climate tolerable, and then it could be very cold.

A cavalryman describes in *The Field* how he sets about it.

'The oorial is a sheep, but in many ways he is curiously goat-like, with his beard, his erect carriage of the head, his jerky movements on a hillside. The colour varies from a dull brown to chestnut. The old rams have a white face, beard and black mane, the body has a black mark behind the withers and shoulder with a whitish saddle patch, the rump and legs are also white. Roughly speaking the older the ram the more white he has about him.

'The day would start with tea and a plate of porridge in the dark, and then a march under the paling sky up a dry water course in the company of two huddled figures, one of which day disclosed as the shikari with red-dyed beard, khaki coat and puttees. The other a silent, wizened, goat-like individual, the tiffin coolie, marvellously excited and a glutton for work. The first pink rays of the sun on the hill tops would find us blowing our fingers in the chill dawn, crouched on the lip of some great corrie. As we watch there comes a touch on the arm, "There they are" says the shikari, "Look, do you see those two white stones?" There are millions of them. "A little to the left is a dark coloured bush." There are thousands of dark coloured bushes. "And there is a female feeding below it." At last a movement of one of the millions of stones catches the eye, and a peep through glasses shows it to be the white rump of a ewe leisurely feeding some seven hundred yards away. A consultation between shikari and Goat Face, during which more ewes and a ram have shown up, then in the field of the glasses up steps the patriarch of the herd and stands at gaze on a rock. A patch of sunlight catches him and shows up the almost complete twin circles of the horns. He is shootable, well over thirty inches. We creep back out of view, start on an endless descent of the incredibly steep mountain side, and arrive, scratched with thorns and with barbed spear grass sticking into every crevice of our clothes, at a point where a shot may be possible. But no, the hillside is empty. After another long look the herd is discovered on the next ridge and the painful process is repeated till we crawl into position at two hundred yards range. The big chap shows up well. How to take the shot? Lie down? There are nothing but knife edged chunks of limestone two feet square to lie on. By the time one had wriggled into some sort of firing position the old boy has browsed himself a yard to the right, and is covered by a bush, while one of his ladies is obviously getting suspicious. At last the moment comes, heart pounds, backsight, foresight and mark are a blur and he is just going to move out of sight over a ridge. Bang, a rattle of stones, and that miracle, a rush of frightened hill game down a precipitous *khud* (hillside) and the whole herd is lost to view. "You missed him" says the shikari. "Damn" says master. A succession of little dots show on the skyline and finally disappear. The last to go, seen through the glasses is the old gentleman moving as gaily as Grandpa Kruschen himself.

'After a morning of this toilsome work we generally find a patch of sunlight, for the wind in the shade strikes chill, and there sit down to talk, remove the spear grass from our persons and eat the midday meal. After a smoke and a long rest in the sun, the noonday hush broken by the whistle of air in the wings of the big vultures, the small noises from the plain came up marvellously clear; the shout of herdsmen, the smack of a woodman's axe, and sometimes the sweet broken melody of a shepherd's pipe, so that one wondered if the goat-footed god himself was abroad in that lonesome place.

'At last the happy toilsome days passed, leave was drawing to an end, and I had registered four clean misses at good heads, my dour old bearer daily becoming more dour, for had he not been spreading tales of the hundreds of tigers I had never shot in the jungles of Central India. Once I had a shot at a patriarch but spared him as he had lost six or eight inches off both his horns. At last there came a day when we crawled round a pinnacle of rock straight into view of some ewes across the way. Recognition was mutual, but instead of bolting they stopped and sneezed, very much as startled chinkara will. There was nothing for it but to crawl back, ever so gradually, out of sight and try for a new point. I cautiously projected my nose, one eye, and the Mannlicher across an upturned slab, one foot planted, the heel of the other tremulously suspended over space. An old ram moved into view. I fired from my horribly insecure position and missed at fifty yards. I fired a snap shot at the ram that followed as the herd bolted and saw him lurch to the shot as he recrossed the skyline. As I was reloading the biggest head I saw on the trip appeared and paused for an instant before he too passed. His horns were thirty six inches if they were an inch. It looked like two more misses. The first was, the second wasn't; for we picked up a dead ram with a twenty nine inch head forty feet down the khud.

'Was it all worth it? Ten very strenuous days, all alone, rising in the dark, much really hard work and discomfort, all to get one pair of moderate sized sheep's horns. It is all a matter of taste. Some people can't go off by themselves without being bored to tears. To others, the lonesome wandering in that high free ground, the joy of seeing wild things, and the hard marching brings peace to the soul, freed for a space from the daily routine of the parade ground, the office and the club.'

# 10. The Himalayas

*The Last Rest House in Lahoul*

When you took your leave shooting in the jungle, at any rate during the last fifty years covered by this book, you probably went to a forest block booked in advance. The difficulties of getting there caused you few headaches, thirty-six hours in the train and a couple of days' march and you were there. You did not move outside the limits of your block, and if you were after tiger there was plenty of other game to shoot or watch in the intervals of pursuing your main objective.

The chapters on jungle shooting have made the point that much of the charm lay in the fact that you were in surroundings quite different from those you knew in cantonment or civil station. If you decided to go up to the Himalayas you went into another world. The name is in general use for the tangled mass of mountains that formed the northern frontier of the old Indian Empire.

A bird's eye view, and a high flying bird at that, of the Great Himalayan Range, using the word in its proper geographical sense, shows that its eastern flank rests on the Brahmaputra river and that it runs continuously north west to Nanga Parbat (26,620 feet), the

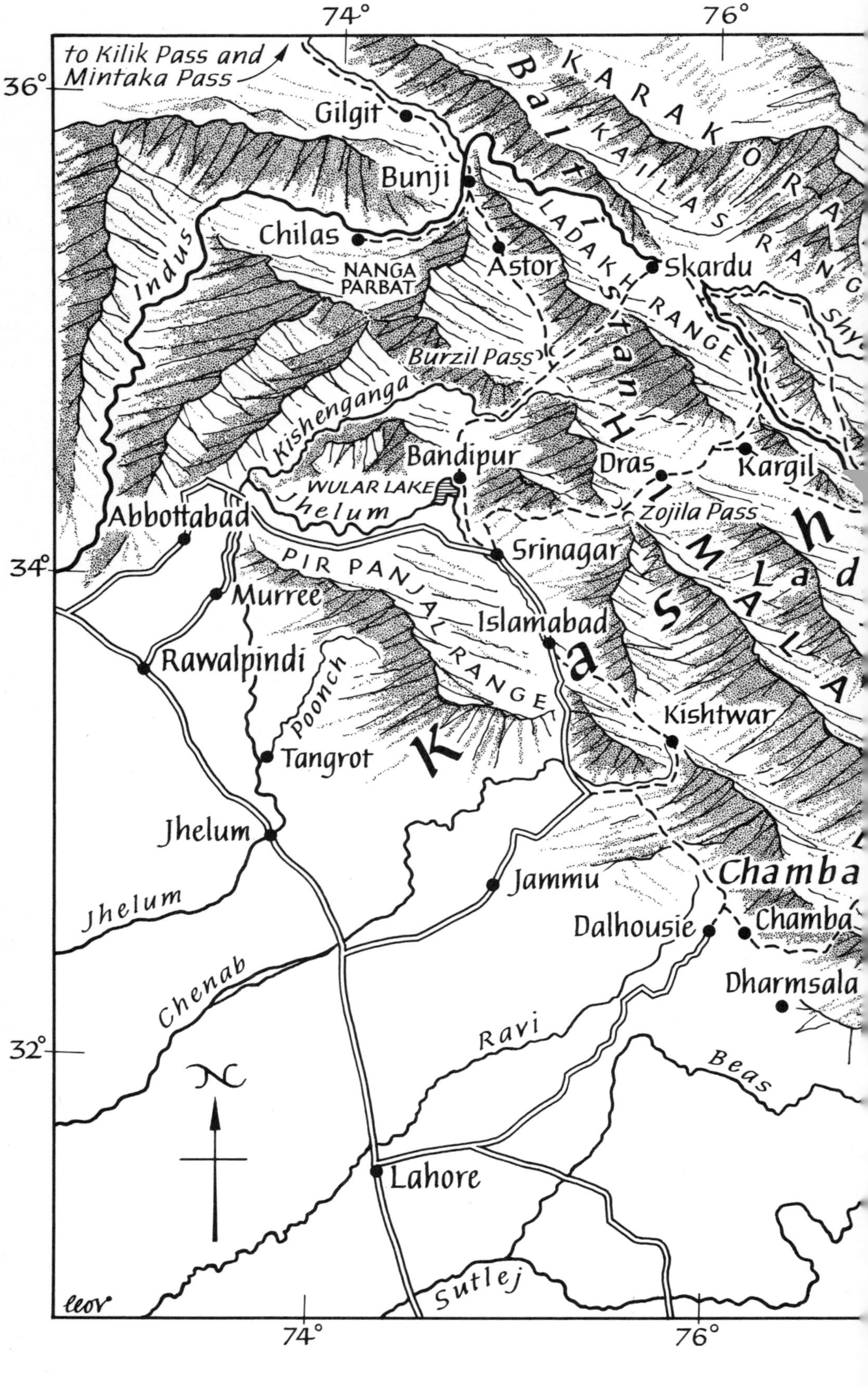

74°
76°
36°
34°
32°
to Kilik Pass and Mintaka Pass
Gilgit
Bunji
Chilas
NANGA PARBAT
Astor
Skardu
KARAKORAM
KAILAS RANGE
LADAKH RANGE
Indus
Burzil Pass
Kishenganga
Bandipur
WULAR LAKE
Jhelum
Dras
Kargil
Zojila Pass
Abbottabad
Srinagar
PIR PANJAL RANGE
Murree
Islamabad
Rawalpindi
Poonch
Kishtwar
Tangrot
Jhelum
Jammu
Chamba
Dalhousie
Chamba
Dharmsala
Jhelum
Chenab
Ravi
Beas
Lahore
Sutlej
leov

78°
80°
36°
34°
32°
he Himalayas and beyond
Motor roads
Tracks
50
100
150
200 Miles
50
100
200
300 Kilometres
CHANG CHEN MO
LADAKH RANGE
Leh
PANGONG TSO
NYAK TSO
Tibet
ZASKAR RANGE
Lachalung Pass
TSO MORARI
Baralacha Pass
velong
Spiti
Rohtang pass
Kulu
KAILAS RANGE
LADAKH RANGE
Indus
Sutlej
imla

great bastion round which the Indus swings south on its final course to the Indian Ocean. It will be seen from the map on the previous pages that the main range has two subsidiaries to the south and one to the north, and that there are three quite separate ranges lying beyond to the north-east.

Taking this snow-clad array of the highest mountains in the world in the order you met them as you came up from the plains of India, the first offshoot forks south-west about longitude 78°. These are the snows that are seen from Simla. They comprise the tiny hill state of Chamba and the districts of Lahoul and Spiti. The other southern branch takes off west of the river Sutlej and peters out south and west of Srinagar when it reaches the Jhelum. It is called the Pir Panjal and continues across the river as the Kaj Nag. Over the Pir Panjal is the famous Vale of Kashmir, covering the source and upper reaches of the river Jhelum. The main Himalayan range runs along the northern edge of Spiti and Lahoul then north and east of Srinagar, and the Zaskar lies between it and the upper waters of the Indus. Over the river you come to the Ladakh range, beyond that to the Kailas, then on to the Karakorum and the Hindu Kush, the extreme northern frontier of the old Indian empire where it marched with Russia and China.

There was game the length and breadth of this vast expanse, but the scope is limited at the eastern end, while the state of Nepal blocks all access to the centre, so we are concerned only with the tract lying north of the valley of the Sutlej.

The hills of the main Himalayas are of primeval granite and the approach to the passes steep and lung testing. Lying at a height of around 12,000 feet, they are closed by snow from October to May. The snow line is as low as 15,000 feet. The further ranges are of softer shale, the approaches more gentle, and although several of the passes stand at 17,000 feet the snowfall is so much lighter that they are closed only in winter. The snow line is around 19,000 feet. The tree line on all ranges is just above the eleven thousand mark.

It is the watershed of the main range that is in every way the most significant of them all, for the simple reason that its southern slopes take the main onslaught of the monsoon clouds and strip them of most of their moisture. The difference is very much more than one of geology. On the day you cross this great divide the contrast of climate and scenery between morning and evening is quite staggering. On the southern side the climate is temperate and bracing, between March and October never too hot or too cold: it was good just to be alive. On the northern side the nights are bitterly cold, even in mid summer the temperature drops to freezing point. By day it soars into a fierce blast of furnace intensity, every rock, stone and grain of sand reflecting the heat back in your face. Instead of the pleasant trek by day you were forced to march through the starlit night, lying up in what shade you might find during the day. As might be expected, the scenery varies with the climate: on the south, steep valleys and tumbling snow-fed streams, well wooded with belts of rhododendron, juniper and silver birch up to the tree line: soft blues and greens with the ever-lasting snows behind. On the north the valleys are wider, the peaks higher and the effect starkly magnificent as opposed to beautiful. To march through the one was sheer joy, through the other you were confronted with a sense of challenge, the general effect was hostile.

The sportsman had the choice of four areas open to him. Taking them in ascending order of the demands made on his physical fitness and prowess as a mountaineer, and on the time available, they were: the vale of Kashmir; Chamba and Lahoul; over the Baralacha Pass from Lahoul to Leh and Ladakh; and from Kashmir over the Zoji La or Burzil passes to Skardu and Baltistan, or to Astore and Gilgit.

Kashmir was the most accessible, and from Srinagar you probably did not have to go more than three or four marches at the most to reach your shooting ground. Chamba was also easy to get at, though the marches into your chosen nullah might be a day or so longer. But if you decided to cross the main range into Central Asia you needed a lot more time.

Along the centuries old trade route it took eighteen days to reach Leh, the great central bazaar where for a few weeks in high summer merchants from India, Tibet, China, Yarkund and Kashgar met to exchange their wares. It took the same number of days to reach it if, when you had crossed the Zoji La, you kept north between Dras and Kargil. The advantage of this pass was that it was clear of snow earlier in the spring than the others, though it was the longer route if you were going to Skardu. If you started later in the year you would use the Burzil which you reached after a two-day trip by houseboat to the Wular Lake. From the lake it took eight days to reach Skardu, seven to Astore, and from there eight days on to Chilas, or five to Gilgit. These were the times along the road to your advanced base. It might take another two days or longer to reach your shooting ground.

Planning was all important. The time of year, the freedom of the passes from snow, the game you hoped to shoot and its seasonal movements, all had to be taken into account. Once over the main range you would be dependent on coolies to carry your baggage, to be engaged from one village to the next along the road, so you had to keep down the weight. At the same time you might be shooting and even sleeping out at heights between 18,000 and 20,000 feet, where the thermometer at night dipped below zero Fahrenheit. It was essential to be well fed, and to have tents, bedding and clothes to keep you warm. And that went, of course, for the servants you took with you. You had to get your sums right, for your chances of success might be much reduced if you had done them wrong.

Within the limits of the time available the first and all important point to decide was what it was you wanted to shoot. A remarkable book was published in 1926, *Big Game Hunting in the Himalayas and Tibet* by Major Gerald Burrard. It bears the same unmistakable stamp of personal knowledge and authority as Dunbar's *Wild Animals in Central India.* Coloured maps give the geographical distribution of all the main species of game and are backed by full information as to their habits. Burrard's advice is quite simple: decide what you want to shoot, then pick an area where you know you may find it. Start with a study of the Survey of India maps on the scale of 16 miles to the inch and narrow the choice down to reasonable proportions; then use the quarter inch map for the final decision.

It was a counsel of perfection but, however you set about it, it is obvious that the more trouble you took in advance, the less time you would waste when you reached your shooting ground. And the more you impressed your shikari with your knowledge, the less likely he would be to try to impose on you.

The professional shikari, or ghillie, was a figure virtually unknown in jungle shooting, but when you reached your base in Srinagar or Chamba, a motley crowd of these characters would be lying in wait for you, armed with sheaves of testimonials from former employers. You would be wise to treat both papers and their owners with great caution. If a man was well shod, with puttees spiralling neatly up to good homespun knickerbockers; if he carried a bandolier, and was girt with a well polished belt holding a couple of skinning knives, you would pass rapidly on to one less pretentious.

Apart from considerable ingenuity in parting you from your money, these men had one thing in common; they would want to take you to a place they knew. If you found that the man you eventually chose disagreed with your choice it was probably because he had never been there, and it could well mean that you had picked a locality that had not been shot over for years.

To some extent, depending on your own experience, the help you needed came under three headings: where to go, how to get there and how to set about stalking and shooting when you arrived. The help that the man you engaged in Srinagar or Chamba could give you was limited to the first two: he would be invaluable in organising, in engaging coolies along the road and in finding a local shikari when you got there. But it was to the latter that you turned for information on terrain and the movements of game and flocks when at last you got down to business.

If the man who had come up with you knew the area, so much the better, but if you were inexperienced, which meant, among other things, that you would not know how far you could rely on him, he might take you for a ride. The less-good ones were not to be trusted when once your quarry had been located. Their one idea, no matter how long the range or improbable the shot, was to persuade you to press the trigger. The ball was then in your court and if you fluffed your shot it was not their fault.

An officer whose ambition was no greater than to shoot a black bear from his base in a houseboat on the Wular Lake, fell into the hands of an ingenious rogue. On a bright moonlight night he was installed in a machan overlooking a patch of Indian corn and told that an enormous black bear, the largest the oldest inhabitant could remember, visited the field every night and played havoc with the crop. The shikari had an accomplice whose imitation of a bear feeding in Indian corn complete with accompaniment of snorts, belches and other rude noises, was held to be the most life-like in the wide vale of Kashmir. His part in the plot was to give his performance from the cover of the standing crop, and after about half an hour, to make off into the forest, and so home. Honour would have been satisfied, and if the sportsman did not get a shot, that was just too bad. But on the night in question the artist was so carried away by the virtuosity of his performance that he broke cover and emerged into the moonlight. He was shot dead.

But there are stories of gallantry in moments of danger, or of nursing a master taken sick a hundred miles from the nearest doctor. Whistler, in *The High Himalayas*, describes a shikari he met in Lahoul:

> 'I found a wisp of a youth leaning lazily against the rail that runs round the Kyelang verandah. . . . I felt very doubtful about his qualifications, for he looked only about sixteen and he lounged there with a wistful air, half sad, half reflective, that seemed more suited to a poet and a dreamer than to one who would help me to circumvent the wily ibex. . . . Yet his appearance belied his capabilities. I was to find out in the three years I knew him that Moti Ram was a born shikari, with an eye like a

hawk, ready to hunt any living thing—ibex or burhel, rose finch or butterfly. . . . On the hillside he was untiring, and his keenness never abated.'

Quite different was Rahim Loon, one of a famous family of Kashmir shikaris; in every way resembling an old markhor, his body like steel, tireless on the hills. He had twice travelled on intelligence duties, Kipling's 'Great Game', from Srinagar to Peking, carrying back his master's notes and messages. The latter took him home to Edinburgh, walked him down Princes Street and then over a deer forest. He returned to Kashmir with but a poor opinion of stalking in Scotland.

When shooting in the hills most people preferred to go alone. In the jungle there was much to be said for company; two rifles were better than one in a beat, invaluable if you had a wounded tiger on your hands. But in the hills he travelled the fastest who travelled alone. Two was a crowd in an ibex nullah; you needed plenty of elbow room, and even if a pair did the approach march together, they would have to split up when they reached their shooting grounds and be independent in terms of tents and cooking arrangements; so there was no real saving in loads. The number of coolies to be found in villages along the road was also limited: they might find enough for one traveller, but not for two.

If you were away for long you had to face the fact that you might tire of your own company. Ronaldshay, who was alone for a trip lasting all told nearly six months, records an unexpected meeting in Skardu with another sportsman after being on his own for nine weeks. Their joy was mutual, they dined together and sat late exchanging experiences, and indeed became so engrossed in doing so that it was only after the stranger had left next morning that he realised he had not even asked his name. He also heard that a friend was somewhere in the area and, as one might shoot an arrow into the air, he sent a note suggesting that they might meet. Two days later the friend arrived for dinner and left the next morning, having walked twenty miles each way to accept the invitation.

There were many details, trivial in themselves, that might make all the difference to your comfort, if not to your health. To help the novice and jog the memory of the experienced there was a small book, *The Sportsman's Vade Mecum*. No trifle was too small for inclusion. How to refine bear's fat and make cold tea and, running down the index, invaluable advice on drawers, flannel vests and Vaseline.

The list of things you would like to take was a long one but every pound counted. Books were a must, but in the days before paperbacks they had to give value for weight. If you ran out of reading material you might be reduced to Kinloch's expedient of learning off by heart the legend on his bottle of sauce. In Victorian days the manufacturer really did tell you what was in the bottle.

# 11. Kashmir and Chamba

*A 'Jhula' Bridge*

The Vale of Kashmir was easily accessible, it was easy to move around within its limits, the scenery was magnificent and your skill and nerve as a mountaineer would be no more severely tested than on a cross country walk on Snowdon or the Cairngorms. And you could ring the changes: two or three weeks' shooting, a fortnight's fishing and you still had ten days left for a few rounds of golf in Gulmarg. But the choice of game was limited. In the summer there was nothing but the black bear, which were not too hard to find in the surrounding foothills, and a few red bear if you went a little further afield. There were, admittedly, markhor in the Pir Panjal and in its continuation across the Jhelum, the Kaj Nag. They offered some really difficult shooting without having to make the long marches across the main range to Astore; but the number of permits granted was limited, and not many went there.

The most sought after game animal of Kashmir was the stag, the barasingh or twelve pointer. They spent the summer, while the stags shed their horns, at higher altitudes but about the middle of September they began to move down and through the winter were found along the valley of the upper Jhelum, from west of the Wular Lake across to the borders of Chamba and Kishtawar. It was said that a stag returned to the same nullah year after year, and it is possible

*Kashmir Stag*

that some never moved away, though in the cover of the dense forests they were seldom seen during what was, of course, the close season. In the early days, before the introduction of the game laws, they were killed indiscriminately by villagers in search of meat: they drove them into snow drifts and set about them with any weapon that came to hand. The antlers are very beautiful, resembling the Scottish red deer, but larger, heavier and more symmetrical. The record head measures $53\frac{1}{2}$ inches along the curves and anything from 40–45 inches was considered good.

There were various ways of finding a stag: one was to camp about the tree line when the first snows fell in September in the hope of finding tracks that would lead to a stalk in the open, or at least to a line to follow to the grazing grounds below. Another was to search the open glades in the forests when the animals were on the move. But there was always an element of luck in shooting a barasingh. You would lose sight of your stag as you moved through the forest, and might well bump into another you did not know was there, so for skill it did not compare with a stalk over open ground after ibex, markhor or ammon. Even so it was no game for those with weak hearts.

> 'The nullah up which we climbed was narrow and strewn with rocks and large boulders which made the going slow and very difficult. As a line of approach it was ideal for its sides were steep enough to shelter us from every wind that blew and, in addition to screen us from view and ensure that the chances of the stag hearing our approach were reduced to an absolute minimum.
>
> 'It took us just over two hours to toil up that rugged ascent and the small mountain stream which tumbled over the rocks and wound its way down into the nullah made the climb extremely precarious so that on several occasions our feet slipped on the moist surface of the rocks and nearly sent us dashing down the mountain side in company with the little stream itself. When we were near the top one of the coolies slipped and loosened a large boulder from its lodging in the nullah bank and a great rock went clattering down to the bottom, and as it bounded from ledge to ledge created sufficient noise in that steep-sided nullah to awaken all the dead in Kashmir, let alone to frighten the stag from the place where he was feeding.
>
> 'However the wind stood us in good stead and although the noise appeared deafening to our ears it apparently did not penetrate as far as the stag's position.

'When we reached the point we had been heading for we scrambled up the sides and crawled along the top keeping just below the crest. The mountain face sloped gently towards the valley below and a little over a hundred yards from where we were the gradient of the surface dropped suddenly to form a convex slope which screened us from the unsuspecting stag. The shikari stopped us while he crept forward to test the wind and locate the stag. A few minutes later he returned and reported that everything was perfect.

'It was all I could do to control my excitement as I took the rifle from one of the coolies and my heart was thumping so furiously that I was almost afraid the stag might hear it despite the force of the wind. Following the shikari I worked my way forward and after half an hour's crawl I came in sight of the beast. He was standing perfectly erect gazing across the nullah with his horns thrown slightly backwards. It was indeed a wonderful sight to watch him standing there, a king among beasts, lord of all he surveyed. As I drew the rifle into my shoulder and aligned the sights I could not help feeling slightly remorseful at taking the life of so magnificent a creature. With a roar the first shot went off. He staggered and his hindquarters collapsed beneath him. I reloaded my rifle, but a second shot was not necessary.' (*The Field*)

The Himalayan black bear is found in Kashmir, in Chamba, and indeed anywhere along the main range where there is thick jungle, as he is an animal of the forest and does not live above the tree line. He is heavily built with the characteristic white V on his chest, and because of the difficulty of the ground on which he lives, more active and aggressive than his cousin, the sloth bear of the jungles of the foothills and plains. He will not, unless provoked, attack a man, but he will kill or inflict terrible injuries upon any luckless woodcutter who stumbles across him and wakes him from his noon-day sleep. He is omnivorous: apart from natural food he is very partial to all cereal crops, mulberries, apricots and walnuts; and he kills cattle. There are plenty of stories of his being shot from a machan as he returned in the approved tiger fashion to feed on the cow he had killed the previous night. In his method of grubbing for roots and insects and in the joy expressed on finding some delicious morsel he resembles the sloth. Burrard remarks that he was less interested in shooting black bears than any other form of Himalayan game, but he never tired of watching them. If bears became numerous in the vicinity of a village they were a scourge to the community and the villagers were always glad to see them shot, and to give information of their whereabouts.

They feed mainly by night, emerging from their caves as the shadows lengthen in the evening and returning as soon as the sun is up. Their actual habits vary with the seasons of the year. In the spring your plan would be to visit grassy open places in the jungle, either very early or about four o'clock, and remain on watch for them to return to or leave their sleeping places. When the crops grew the bears would move down, and later still when the apricots and walnuts ripened, the orchards were certain to attract them and they would climb trees to get at the fruit and nuts. There was one golden rule. Never shoot a bear in a tree, particularly if you were standing underneath it. You could not be sure just which part of his anatomy you were aiming at, and if hit he was likely to drop like a stone to the ground, recover his balance with remarkable agility, and start looking round for the cause of the trouble.

The Himalayan red bear is the same animal as the brown bear of Europe. He lives above the tree line with a preference for the grassy slopes of ranges whose tops are capped with snow. They are found mostly in Chamba and Kashmir, and they hibernate for four months from mid November.

Their favourite feeding grounds are the patches of lush green grass of old sheepfolds and their main diet is grass, roots and grubs. They might be attended by flocks of crows waiting for the pickings they leave behind, and the presence of these birds might betray a bear's whereabouts. On the other hand they have an ally in the monal pheasant which is plentiful on red bear ground. 'No finer game bird flies but they are perfect fiends for getting up with a great whir and sailing down the khud uttering shrill cries. It is as difficult to elude the vigilance of a monal as of a peacock, and all other animals know and understand its warning.'

Although mostly inoffensive enough in their tastes, they are not above eating carrion and there is a gruesome story of two men, overwhelmed by an avalanche on the Burzil, whose bodies were eaten by red bears before they were found by the search party sent out in the spring. If they do acquire a liking for flesh they can be a scourge to the flocks who come up to graze during the summer months.

Although they are generally harmless they needed the protection given them by the restriction on the numbers permitted to be shot on a game license.

In terms of difficult shooting, Chamba, giving access to Lahoul, was a halfway house between Kashmir on the one hand and Ladakh

Baltistan on the other. Shooting blocks were allotted by the State and were seldom more than four or five marches from the capital. The peaks did not rise to more than 20,000 feet, but they were of incredible steepness and the valleys very tight. You would find yourself in surroundings of great beauty. At a height of 11,000 feet, in air of champagne quality, your camp might lie in a wide green meadow carpeted with flowers of every colour. From your tent door there would be a view of a stream tumbling down through a maze of chestnuts, walnuts, firs and deodars. Behind, the snows rose to 20,000 feet; to the right a view of a magnificent glacier, wildly grand and impressive; to the left a valley where the stream, even in June, was completely bridged over by snow.

Apart from the red bear, the game animals were the thar and the gooral, who lived below the snow line. Their heads are less impressive than ibex or markhor, but they lived on ground of precipitous difficulty: slopes as steep as 60° made perilous by carpets of pine needles and slippery turf. The shrubs that grew on them served the dual purpose of providing a hand hold and concealing from the eye the perils that lay below. In the north part of Chamba and on into Lahoul you might find the burhel, the wild sheep of Tibet, and a few ibex, though the latter were so small as to be hardly worth shooting.

In the early days there was game also in Kulu, which lies south-east of Chamba and south of the Rohtang pass leading into Lahoul, but an over generous issue to the villagers of gun licenses for crop protection resulted in its annihilation. There is an account of shooting in Kulu in *How I shot my Bears* by Mrs Tyacke.

The choice of the singular pronouns is significant. For the benefit of any other lady who might think of following her she offers advice on suitable clothes. 'A very short plain skirt'—the accompanying illustration shows that it ends a good hand's breadth above the ankle—'in strong *karkee* drill, not too narrow as it would interfere with the jumping and climbing over the rocks that is so often necessary'. On setting out, she discarded her Champion and Wilton saddle and Busvine habit and took to riding astride after the manner of the Kulu ladies. For bedtime she advises a very warm bed jacket and pyjamas. What her husband thought of all this she does not record, he was very much the junior partner. One evening when he had failed to shoot a red bear he came back 'exceedingly ashamed of himself, to receive a most severe lecture from me for having been so foolish as to throw away such a chance'.

When they decided to move on into Lahoul only three of their coolies could be bribed into going with them. 'One was a fool, one an idiot and the third a convict, so it will be easily imagined how

*Gooral Country*

much menial work fell on my shoulders.' On another occasion quite late in the day news was brought in of a panther in the jungle below the camp. Her husband protested that it was not worth going down 1,500 feet just on chance. 'But I, who have twice the "go" he has, insisted on starting at once. I was longing for a shot at "spots".'

Gooral and thar, the main attraction for the sportsman in Chamba, are essentially Himalayan animals. Their territories overlap and they might be found on the same ground. Neither live above the tree line, but the thar will not go as low as the gooral, the gooral will not care to venture into the rugged precipices favoured by the thar. If it was the latter you were after you would scan with your glasses the wildest and most inaccessible crags. The gooral is known for his 'devil-may-care Alpine work'; it is said that while the ibex climbs as a matter of duty the thar climbs for fun.

The pursuit of both of them was a game for the man with a steady head for heights. Looking back across some almost precipitous slope, clad in slippery turf, which you had crossed in the excitement of the chase, you might reflect that you would never have attempted it in cold blood. And time and again in books on this branch of sport one comes across remarks of which this is typical: 'I have frequently had to walk along the side of a precipice with nothing to step on but my shikari's hands and head. How he was supported I do not know.'

Weight for weight, the gooral resembles the chamois but the horns lack the distinctive hook of the Alpine animal. They are to be found on precipitous slopes and khuds covered with undergrowth and though they do not mind the heat they are intolerant of sun and unless on shady ground, they feed only in the early morning and evening. Their natural colouring blends so perfectly with their surroundings that they are hard to pick up even with glasses.

In Himalayan shooting, under no circumstances was it practicable to drive game up to the rifle. If for any reason a stalk was impossible, the only thing was to wait till next day when the animals might have moved to more favourable ground. Burrard tells the story of his first ever attempt at Himalayan shooting. Only one day's march out from his base, in a locality where he expected to find nothing, a villager introduced himself as a shikari and asked if he wished to shoot a gooral. A bargain was struck: if he was shown a gooral he was to pay a rupee. No gooral, no money. Early next morning at the foot of a long slope, with a clump of pines at the top, the man halted and pointed out two gooral. The stalk did not appear to be unduly difficult, but the objection was made that the animals would very soon leave their feeding grounds and that a drive was the better plan. The man pointed out, and it was no more than the truth, that he could reach their level far more quickly if he went alone, and that he knew exactly which way they would move if disturbed. They would come down past a certain boulder and if the sahib would take up a position accordingly he would undoubtedly shoot one if not both of them. It sounded so plausible, but the result was a fiasco. The gooral followed the predicted path, but at a pace which made any chance of a shot out of the question. They came down the khud like rockets. 'The shikari expressed his regret, I curbed my disappointment, and he got his rupee.'

Burrard later met an old gentleman who had retired to live in the nearby hill station and his suspicions were confirmed. The gooral were the only two surviving in the locality, and they provided a small but steady income for the shikari.

The thar is a goat, heavily built, a full grown buck standing nine to ten hands at the shoulder and weighing up to 200 lb. The hair on the head is short and there is no beard, but they have a long mane reaching nearly to the knees. The remarkable thing is that the thar, in size and body weight little smaller than the ibex, should have such insignificant horns. Although the horn is extremely thick at the base the record is only just over 15 inches compared with over 50 inches of the ibex. This may account for it being held in little esteem. Victorian sportsmen with plenty of room on the walls of billiard rooms and baronial halls, went in search of something more impressive.

To judge the merits of the thar as a game animal only on the size of his horns is to overlook two points very much in his favour. He was plentiful and he was to be found over a wide range of territory on the southern slopes of the main Himalayan range from about the centre of the Pir Panjal as far east as you chose to go. This meant that you could shoot a thar without the expenditure of time and money involved on a trip to Baltistan in search of ibex, a point of some importance to the subaltern who was hard up or had only a limited period of leave. The other point is that if the true criterion of worth of a trophy is the difficulty to be overcome in securing it, then the thar comes very near the top of the list.

> 'The obstacles which hamper the successful pursuit of the thar are so great that I prize his trophy beyond very many others of species which are usually considered more noble game. And the memories which each head recalls are pleasanter than those conjured up by almost any other head.'

The thar lived among the steepest precipices, leaving them only with reluctance in search of food. He liked the shade, and would lie up by day in thick scrub from which he would emerge only in the evenings. It called for all your experience and skill to locate him, and the stalk that followed would test to the limit your reserves of fitness, nerve and determination. When the critical moment came, with your feet supported by your shikari in the only position from which you could take a shot, you might look down to a river foaming along 3,500 feet below you. On the whole it was better not to look. It might not be a sheer drop, but you would not bounce many times.

# 12. Sheep and Goats

*Ferry Across the Indus*

As has been said, when you crossed the main Himalayan Range and headed for the Indus you passed into another world: a world where the elements, wind, frost and snow, had to be taken into account in almost every plan you made and might even endanger your life. As civilisation understands the words, there were no roads or paths and you had to follow and outwit animals whose home lay among crags and precipices at a height where the very act of putting one foot in front of another was a burden. You had to be superlatively fit or you would be in no state to take the shot when it came after a stalk that might have lasted a couple of days.

You went, of course, with a clear-cut idea of what you were hoping to do. In very general terms, Ladakh, with its capital at Leh, was a land of high open plateaus, the home of the sheep: the ovis ammon and the burhel. As the Indus flowed west to swing round Nanga Parbat the mountains closed in, and in Baltistan, Gilgit and Astore you found the goats: the ibex and the markhor.

It is remarkable at what an early date the first sportsmen found their way into this remote unmapped region. There is a mention of Ladakh as early as 1850, only a year after the Second Sikh War opened the Punjab to the British, and it was probably reached by following the well-worn trade route to Leh. General Kinloch, in *Large Game Shooting in Thibet and the North-West*, refers to a 'Cashmere Route Map' with the help of which 'the intending traveller may easily find out how long it will take him to reach the ground he desires to hunt over'. On maps in use sixty years later, much of the information was based on those early surveys. He mentions a Mr Wilson, 'the well-known shikari', who had already shot extensively over the whole region. Kinloch was a subaltern in The Rifle Brigade and he followed up his first visit in 1861, which he regarded as a reconnaissance, with others in 1862, 1864 and 1866, all lasting as long as six months. One infers that he was on good terms with his commanding officer who may, of course, have found life more peaceful in the absence of such a restless and enterprising officer. In between his journeys Kinloch found time to write his book, the accuracy of which is still unchallenged on points of geographical and zoological fact. In 1864 he complains that the region had been spoilt by the incursion of tourists.

Whichever route you chose you might very soon have a foretaste of what you had let yourself in for. The trade route to Leh crossed at a very early stage the Rohtang Pass above the source of the river Beas. It cuts through a range where the main peaks are over 20,000 feet, by a gap at just over 13,000 feet. It is completely closed from December to March and for a further six weeks on either side of that period it may be crossed only by the most hardy, unburdened by any packs. As late as May in one year 200 travellers were overwhelmed by an avalanche. At any season there is a fearsome wind which without the help of any of the other elements can close the pass for hours on end. As far as the Baralacha Pass, over the main range, the Indian Government maintained a road to a standard fit for pack animals. With its historical connections there was more incident to interest the traveller than on either of the routes that started from Kashmir. You met caravans of Tibetans and Ladakhis coming south to barter wool in Kulu, their Mongol faces and greasy pigtails proclaiming their origin. Rosy-cheeked Lahoula mountaineers in practical brown home-spun; Hindu muleteers straggling along in unpractical dirty white garments, their shins exposed to the biting winds, blankets huddled round their necks. Whistler records that he met a sadhu on the pass, in thin saffron robe and clogs, 'who mumbled sadly of the cold and the horror of the snow'.

Two marches beyond the Rohtang stood the castle of the Hindu ruler of Lahoul, frowning on the caravans as they toiled along the road; a vantage point in the stormy history of the little state.

> '. . . even in days of peace eyed with grave concern by all who passed, wondering if some unseen sentinel had sent a message to his lord that here was food for plunder, a bale of cloth, a bag of

> grain, a fine fat sheep, a pretty daughter—what was the tax and pleasure of the Lord of the Road?'

At Tando where the road from Chamba came in, there was a monastery which paid a yearly tribute of thirty rupees to the abbot of the Stagna monastery in Ladakh. He sent it to his superior somewhere in Chinese Tibet, and from him it went to an abbot in Bhutan, exalted in the Buddhist hierarchy as Lord over them all.

At Patseao at the foot of the Baralacha, where at a height of 12,500 feet there may still be snow in July, there is a fair where wool, barley, wheat, salt and borax are bartered. Whistler saw

> 'a Ladakhi woman. Burned and tanned by the fierce seasons of Ladakh she was hideous in the extreme in features, but her long brown gown and trousers formed an effective background to the silver utensils and ornaments that hung from the girdle at her waist. On her head was the berak, with its red serge and massive lumps of turquoise, while the black lappets of fur stood out beside her cheeks.'

On the plain beyond the Baralacha where marmot and snow-cock reign supreme through the long days of snow and frost, and there are no human beings other than the caravans of traders and shepherds who pass through in summer, there is a famous landmark, the Great Stone. A giant boulder standing in lonely solitude, it has been used as a boundary pillar, and on its top are carved the initials 'K/B', for this is where British and Kashmir territory met.

If you reach Leh, the great exchange and mart along the road, in June you will find the place almost empty, but three months later, in *Sport and Politics under an Eastern Sky*, the Earl of Ronaldshay found that

> 'the main street and bazaar was alive with merchants from all parts of Asia: Yarkundis with numdahs, felts, furs and skins; Hindus with cloth and finery from Delhi; Tibetans with turquoises, drugs and tea from Lhasa—all jostling one another and forming a polyglot crowd both striking and picturesque.'

There are two passes out of Kashmir: the Burzil that carries the road to Astore and Gilgit, and the Zoji La, after crossing which you fork, beyond Dras, right for Leh and left for Skardu. The stages to the latter are eight days longer than over the Burzil, but it is open about a month earlier in the year than either of the others. Ronaldshay travelled over the Zoji La, the pass dominated by a mocking fiend of a wind, in the middle of March which was early by any standards, but he was in a hurry to get to Leh. On reaching the hut at the foot of the pass he made his preparations for the evening meal then went out to prospect.

> 'There was a fearful gale blowing, and it is this wind that is one of the chief difficulties to be encountered. . . . However an old post-runner volunteered the information that it frequently dropped towards midnight or in the early hours of the morning, with which consolation we retired after an early dinner.'

When he woke the next morning at 4 a.m. it was still blowing a hurricane, with no sign of it dropping. Nothing daunted, he took two coolies and started on his journey. The gorge leading to the pass was steep and narrow, and many feet deep in snow, which presented an almost perpendicular wall up which they had to cut their way. However, they made it and he records that he had the 'proud distinction of being the first European across the pass that year'.

He returned that way at the end of September.

> 'What a wonderful difference there was. . . . Then it was simply a huge conglomerated mass of snow, whereas now it presented a scene of unparalleled magnificence. All the trees, excepting of course the firs, were clothed in every shade of colour, from a deep copper to a brilliant gold, the whole place was one mass of lovely vegetation. The difference between this beautiful southern side of the pass and the scene of indescribable desolation presented by the northern side, which is innocent of any vegetation whatsoever, is one of the most striking things I have ever seen. I could hardly believe on reaching the Kashmir side I could be within a few hours' walk of the country I had just left '

After a month among the fleshpots of Srinagar he was off again in November, bound for Astore. The road that leads over the Burzil starts from the Wular Lake and zigzags up five thousand feet through a magnificent pine forest, the view dominated by the mighty peak of Haramukh, 'clad in eternal snow, standing out bold and awe-inspiring amid a host of smaller satellites'. In the spring of 1921, the second resthouse, as the road drops to the valley of the Kishenganga, was demolished by an avalanche. It had been built on a small flat opposite a side nullah which, too impatient to wait for its winter load of snow to be melted by the sun, shrugged off the whole mass: snow and stones thundered across the valley and razed the building to its foundations. Ten miles further on, the road turns right past stretches of trout fishing, then up towards the pass where the Burzil stream comes tumbling down in a series of limpid, blue-green pools.

> 'As I ascended the pass the snow became deeper till when I reached the summit it must have lain to a depth of two or three feet. On the highest point of the pass stands a hut firmly built on a stout pedestal of stone to keep the floor above the level of the snows, and in it were one or two mail-runners awaiting the post-bag from Gilgit. Stern, silent-looking men, and no wonder; for the life they lead, cut off from the haunts of men, battered by the storms amid the wild mountains, through the raging winter, where the snow falls to a depth of twenty feet, carrying their lives in their hands, is hardly one to inspire merriment.'

He spent a couple of months shooting markhor, then early in January he received news that for private reasons made it expedient for him to return to civilisation at an early date. He was lucky to survive the journey for it was a foolhardy undertaking. The winter storms that tear down the Burzil at over 13,000 feet, sweep all before them with overwhelming fury. On January 18th he crossed the pass, several feet under snow, with comparative ease but one march down the weather changed. His guide told him that he would reach the next hut, twelve miles away, so they set out with dense masses of ugly cloud rolling ominously towards them. They reached the hut, but towards nightfall a gale sprang up and he spent a wretched, sleepless night wondering what had happened to his coolies. Only a few days before, a telegraph linesman with a party of seven had been overwhelmed by an avalanche, from which only one man emerged alive. His men did in fact trickle in, in twos and threes, but he was stormbound for three days and nights, and could not resume his journey to Srinagar till the 24th.

If you took the right hand road before crossing the Burzil you went to Skardu across a high plateau which was also snow bound till late in the spring. When clear, it emerged as a weird bleak region with all the rugged solitude of Dartmoor on a very much larger scale. A series of rolling downs, strewn with rock and stones, not a tree or a bush for forty miles. A little grass near the streams, 'and here and there patches of onions'. The only living animals are red bear, marmots and, from late morning till mid-afternoon, millions of mosquitoes. One sportsman was driven by their torment to march straight across it without stopping. The marmot is a rodent not unlike a large otter that sits at the mouth of its hole, uttering a shrill, petulant alarm whistle, ready to dart in at the least sign of danger. Unless killed stone dead they succeeded in diving into their holes, and indeed there was no point in shooting them as the skin was so greasy and the fur so harsh as to render it useless.

On the road to Leh once over the Baralacha, you might come across the occasional long strip of cultivation along the banks of stream or river where irrigation was possible, and this would be a real oasis in the desert: crops of barley and peas, vines, and groves of walnut, apricot, mulberry, poplar and willow. Otherwise it was a barren land.

> 'In front sand, behind sand, and on each side sand. Overhead a brazen sky from which blazed down the sun with pitiless fury. Far as the eye could see lay masses of dry burned-up sand, broken here and there by huge mountains of shale and gravel, resembling nothing so much as monster ash-heaps.'

The people of Ladakh took their religion from the Hindu/Buddhist monasteries, but in Baltistan they were Mohammedans of a rough and ready type, dominated by their feudal chiefs. A great feature were the games of polo. The ponies were Badakshani stallions, the ground was enclosed by a three-foot wall so that the ball was always in play, and there were no rules. It was an exciting game, even for the spectator.

There were plenty of natural hazards along the road. If you had to cross a river, the Indus or the Shyok, there were no bridges and you were dependent on the ferry, the 'zuk'. This consisted of twenty or thirty inflated goatskins lashed together with a flimsy decking which was permanently awash. The crew would be five or six men, three or four with long poles to fend the craft off the rocks and swirling shallows, the others equally usefully employed in blowing up the skins, which were far from airtight. To transport a single sportsman with his baggage might take a whole day as the fast flowing stream would carry the raft as much as half a mile downstream on each trip.

The heat was excessive, but the real test of nerve and fortitude came when you reached a defile where the mountains closed in and a spur fell sheer to the bed of the river. You had two choices, You could go up and over, a climb of say 2,000 feet if you were lucky, or a detour of a day or two if you struck a really difficult spot. Or you could take the direct route, using the primitive path built along the face of the cliff.

It is something of a mystery how these contraptions were built, though the basic idea was simple enough. Stakes were driven into any convenient crevice in the rock and were connected by rough beams on which were laid flagstones, forming a 'sort of staircase'. A crazy pavement, if ever the word meant anything. It was not unusual as you crossed and placed a foot on a tread, for it to tip up, affording an excellent view of a sheer drop of a few hundred feet into a foaming torrent below. One traveller on reaching camp after a more than usually perilous passage, consulted his shaving mirror to reassure himself that his hair had not turned grey. He remarks, 'on a road like this, with the June sun on one's back, one asks if it is good enough on the off chance of a shot at a buck goat'.

But in the very starkness of the scenery there was a savage beauty.

> 'Not even the word painting of a Ruskin could do justice to the magical effect of light and vivid colouring among the wonderfully tinted hills of Thibet through the medium of an atmosphere compared with which that of Italy is foggy.'

Kinloch goes on to describe the scenery on the shores of an immense lake south of the Chang Chen Mo.

> 'The hills which slope down to the waters are low and rounded. They are of almost every hue, brown, red, purple, pink, orange, yellow and grey and when seen reflected in the deep blue waters of the lake, form a picture which, if produced on canvas, would be pronounced unreal by those who had never seen the original. Owing to the wonderful clearness of the air every outline is as sharp, every tint as vivid at a distance of twenty miles, as if only a mile away.'

He sums up its charm, despite the bleak appearance and the severe climate,

> 'One there experiences a sensation of perfect freedom which I have never felt elsewhere; and a sort of mystery still hangs over the country, which modern geographical researches have stripped from almost every other country in the world.'

That was written in 1869: how much truer of sixty years later. And Kinloch was not the only one to fall under the spell. Ronaldshay for example.

'Often as I toiled over the huge burnt-up wastes, with no tittle of success to reward my efforts, scorched by the burning noonday sun, chilled by the bitter blasts by night, fed on the unappetising productions of a Kashmiri cook, more unsavoury than ever since dung had become the only fuel available, I wondered wherein lay the extraordinary attraction which drew me willy-nilly from the comforts and luxuries of modern life to wander solitary over the dreary tracts of this forbidding land.'

The hope that at any moment a beast worthy of all the hardship and trouble might be stalked and shot? That had something to do with it, but there was more to it than that. The unfettered freedom of the desert? The subtle fascination of the solitude of nature? He admits that it was something he could not really explain.

## THE SHEEP

The smallest of the sheep is the oorial, alias shapoo, the name by which he is known in Ladakh and Baltistan where he is to be found all along the main valley of the Indus from Leh westwards. No one ever travelled all that way just to shoot a shapoo, but if you were in those parts and were not pressed for time you might well take a few days off to look for him. The open downlands on which he lived were comparatively easy going, but he was lively and suspicious and presented a very worth while challenge to anyone who set out to stalk him.

The next in size is the burhel: standing about nine hands and weighing 150 lb, the horns of the mature ram have a distinct backward curve which has led to his being described as half way between sheep and goat. He is the wild sheep of Tibet and has a wide distribution. From about longitude 77° he lives astride the main Himalayan range, then away to the north-east across the Zaskar and Ladakh and beyond. The grazing on the Himalaya is very much better, for the Zaskar and Ladakh are almost devoid of vegetation, with very little but patches of coarse grass and moss to supplement the ubiquitous dwarf shrub, the *boortza*. But perhaps because the shale and loose rock impart some element to his diet that is lacking in the granite of the main range, it is a fact that the burhel on his native heath carries incomparably the finer head.

For the beginner who wanted to shoot a burhel, it was necessary only to cross the Baralacha pass on the road to Leh; but he would not get a large head. If he was more ambitious, he would make a trip to the Zaskar or Ladakh ranges with burhel as his main objective and by a careful study of the map, stand a chance of shooting a really fine head. On the main range, the snow line kept him down to around 13,000 feet and camp might be pitched in a grassy glade with no shortage of wood for the camp fire. Further afield, the tops of the hills were his limit, and at that level the extra 5,000 feet made a lot of difference.

Zoologically there is little difference between the two great sheep, *Ovis poli*, named after the great explorer the first European to discover it, and *Ovis hodgsoni*, generally though wrongfully known as the ammon. The body of the latter is slightly larger; and a full-grown ram stands twelve hands at the shoulder and may weigh 225 lb. On the other hand, although the ammon head is heavier in girth, the known record is only just over 50 inches, whereas the longest pair of poli horns, presented to Lord Roberts by the Amir of Afghanistan, measure $75\frac{1}{2}$ inches over the curves. And over a doorway next to the library of the Royal Central Asian Society hangs a head measuring 72 inches. It was given to Lord Wavell and by him presented to the Society, which has taken the horns as their crest, over the motto *Cornua levat super terras*. The horns of the ammon make a circle, those of the really big poli form a spiral of considerably more than a circle. The full-grown ram is a majestic sight.

The home of the ammon is in Tibet, but he was found on the Ladakh range and on the northern slopes of the Zaskar. The poli lives on the Pamirs in Chinese Turkestan, and crosses on to Indian territory over the Killik and Mintaka passes only in the tiny state of Hunza. This was several marches beyond Gilgit, and as such beyond the reach of the ordinary sportsman on leave. *Ovis poli* have seldom been shot except by officers of the Indian Political Service or the little garrison of Gilgit.

The ammon seldom comes down below 14,000 feet and in the summer you might have to go over 18,000 feet to find him. He lives on wide open plains, bare of cover, with fickle, shifting winds, where his phenomenally acute senses of sight and smell have full scope to warn him of impending danger. And once warned his long legs carry him away at a gallop to pastures new, so far away that you have no idea of where to start looking for him. It could be goodbye for ever. Except in the rutting season, the rams with warrantable heads lived together in small parties of half a dozen which made them all the harder to approach.

For all these reasons the ammon was the most difficult of all animals to stalk. There were two golden rules to guide you. The first, on windy, gusty days to stay in camp; the second, having chosen a likely area, to search minutely every nook and cranny. It was only too easy to overlook a fold in the ground you never suspected was there, but which was large enough to hide what you were looking for.

Burrard describes a successful stalk at a height of just over 15,000 feet. He had been on the move since dawn and at one o'clock was just about to have his lunch of 'chappati and burhel sandwiches washed down by cold tea', when his shikari, with the naked eye, spotted six ammon feeding on a ridge two miles away. The 40 × telescope showed that they were big rams.

> 'All thoughts of food vanished and I instructed Chiang to remain where he was with the pony, which was laden with the remains of our food and my cast clothes, for the thermometer had indicated 35 degrees of frost when we left camp, and now the sun was so hot we had been sitting in our shirt sleeves.'

After a long detour, with several checks to verify his position, by four o'clock he reached a point where he could turn down a nullah parallel with the one where he had last seen the rams. At that moment the wind, which had been constant from the south-west began to shift and change. After about half an hour 'it stopped its antics' and settled down to blow from the south-east. He had just started to move when four more ammon, two ewes and two small rams, appeared from nowhere and forced him to halt. After a pause, he was just starting for the point from which he hoped to get his shot, when a whisper from the shikari made him look up. The two parties of ammon had joined forces and were standing looking at him from a nullah 250 yards away. He knew that in a moment they would be off.

> 'A quick look through the glasses showed that the left hand one carried horns with massive tips. I took a quick aim and fired. Then ensued one of the finest sights I have ever seen. Off went those ten ammon at full gallop: it was like the start for the Derby. I felt my bullet had gone over the ram's back. Another cartridge was slipped in and the lever slammed home. It was the work of a second. I swung clear of my ram's shoulder as he stretched at full speed up the nullah. This time there was no doubt, for he staggered and started moving downhill away from the others. At a third shot he collapsed in a heap.'

But the day was not yet over. They were still skinning and cutting up the ammon when Chiang arrived to say the pony had broken loose and bolted back to camp.

'This was indeed cheerful news, for the sun was dropping, I was beginning to get bitterly cold and I knew this was nothing to what it would be in a couple of hours' time. I had had nothing to eat since a few mouthfuls snatched during a brief halt at about 10 a.m., and I realised I was very hungry. My warm wraps as well as the food were on the pony so I looked forward to a joyful tramp back to camp, which was anything from 10 to 15 miles away.'

However about 6.30 the pony was caught and after putting on their discarded clothing and eating their interrupted tiffin the party started again for camp. 'We reached it at 10 p.m., just sixteen hours after we had left in the morning. It was one of the longest and most tiring, but also one of the most exciting days of my life.'

Substantially the same problems confronted the sportsman who went after *Ovis poli*, and the climatic conditions were likely to be far more severe. In his poem, *The Feet of the Young Men*, from *The Five Nations*, Kipling describes the pursuits which, over the world, in his judgment present the most exacting challenge to youth. This is the fourth question he asks:

'Do you know the world's white roof-tree, do
  you know the windy rift
Where the baffling mountain eddies chop and change?
Do you know the long day's patience, belly down
  on frozen drift,
While the head of heads is feeding out of range?
It is there that I am going, where the boulders
  and the snow lie,
With a trusty, nimble tracker that I know.
I have sworn an oath, to keep it on the Horns
  of Ovis Poli,
And the Red Gods call me out and I must go!'

In his book *Sport and Life in Further Himalaya*, Kennion throws a little more light on what you had to put up with. He had pitched his camp in 'as dreary a spot as any in Asia', a snowy plain relieved only by patches of green and blue that marked the course of a frozen stream. Leaving in the morning after a breakfast of mutton chops smoked over an unsavoury fire, and tea that froze while he drank it, he was met by a cutting wind like a blast from the North Pole. He began a stalk but it was frustrated, 'when a gale became a blizzard. Undulating curtains of fine, hard snow swept and lashed the ground with indescribable fury. Between gusts, you might see, to aim was impossible. Unprotected the eyes could not be opened in the teeth of the blizzard, goggles were coated with snow in an instant.'

Neither of the two record herds mentioned was actually shot. By a cruel trick of Nature the largest rams are the ones most liable in winter to become bogged down in snow drifts by the weight of their enormous horns. They fall an easy prey to wolves and the heads are picked up later. The one given to Lord Wavell first came into the hands of the late Col. Evelyn Cobb when he was political agent in Gilgit. He had been negotiating an international postal service between India and Chinese Turkestan by way of the Mintaka pass. Not without an ulterior motive, he had by gifts and judicious hospitality, been softening up the Chinese amban who was his opposite number. When the latter expressed a wish to make some return Cobb, who had been told by Kirghiz graziers that the head of an enormous poli, killed by wolves, was lying out at the head of a nearby valley, asked that the men should be ordered to bring the trophy into him. It was some months before the snow cleared sufficiently for them to find it, but they eventually brought in three magnificent heads, measuring 55, 60 and $72\frac{1}{2}$ inches.

The wolves that prey on the ammon and poli are animals of the open plains and are a terrible scourge to animal life, wild or domestic. In their rocky fastnesses the ibex and markhor have another enemy, the snow leopard. With his thick yellowish-grey fur, the dark rings showing like sooty thumb marks, he is the most beautiful of the great cats. They are extremely destructive but as they only come out of their caves after dark they are seldom seen, and as they are not found below the tree line the temperature at night does not encourage sitting up, even when a kill is found. You would indeed be very lucky if you ever saw one. Cosmo Stewart, when with the Mountain Battery in Gilgit, shot an ibex late one evening and had to leave it out for recovery the next day. He got back at dawn and surprised two snow leopards on the kill. And here is another story:

'We had begun to make our way back towards camp when the shikari pointed to some snow leopard tracks which he said were quite fresh. He was very excited so I followed with my rifle at the ready. The tracks led to ground where the short grass gave place to rocks. A few minutes later we came to a burhel kill which seemed to be the work of leopards on the preceding night.

The sturdy little hillman bristled with excitement like a terrier. But for the mist I too felt we might have seen a leopard at any moment. We advanced very cautiously towards some huge rocks. All at once came a loud hiss from my shikari and I swung round and looked in the direction he was pointing. About forty yards away and dimly discernible in the mist a leopard was walking slowly across a large, sloping slab of rock. I took a snap shot, and the leopard disappeared. We scrambled forward and as we neared the edge of the rock there was a noise of falling stones and a leopard showed for an instant between two rocks and then vanished. I cursed my luck feeling sure that I had missed, but the shikari asserted confidently that this was another, and that my shot had been good, and in a few yards he was proved right. My leopard lay stone dead beyond the big rock. We had been lucky enough almost to get a right and left at these wary beasts.' (*The Field*)

## THE GOATS

When after the Old Shikaris annual dinner in Valhalla the talk gets round to the respective merits of the ibex and the markhor as game animals, it is certain that hot words will fly. It may even be that Odin, from his seat at the end of the table, will intervene to part Ward from Kinloch, restore order and give the casting vote. In the difficulty of ground they frequent, their wariness and the methods employed to stalk them, they have so much in common that it is invidious for a mere mortal to claim precedence for either.

There are considerable areas where you may find one without the other but they share a common block of mountainous territory in Astore, Baltistan, Gilgit and Chitral.

The Indian ibex is the largest in the world. He stands about ten hands and his scimitar shaped horns diverge and sweep backwards and downward, the curve towards the back being the distinctive mark of a good head. The record measures 55 inches. The hair is coarse and brittle with in winter a soft undercoat from which the famous Kashmir shawl is spun and woven. The mature buck has a long black tufted beard. The ibex has been described as 'lord of the mountain tops, looking every inch the monarch of all he surveys' but the same writer, Stone, says of the markhor 'a venerable buck standing solitary on a rock contemplating the world below him will make the blood of the most blasé tingle in his veins; or a herd of longbearded seniors, gravely crossing a patch of snow, perhaps just out of range, is a sight that will recur to the mind many a year after.'

*Sheep and Goats*

(top) *Ovis poli*; (left) *Ibex*; (right) *Narkhor*; (bottom) *Thar*

The markhor has a much wider distribution than the ibex. His territory extends from Astore through the whole sweep of the North-West Frontier beyond Waziristan down to Baluchistan. He is the lighter animal of the two and has a copious beard down to his chest. The horns are larger, the record being 63 inches. They have the peculiarity that they vary considerably in type, and geographical names have been given to distinguish them. At one extreme, the Suleiman or Baluchistan head has straight heavily twisted horns, while at the other extreme the Astore has an open horn with both spiral and twist. The Pir Panjal animal is akin to the Astore, the Kabul to the Suleiman. But just to make it more confusing, the types are not restricted to the areas after which they have been named. The Pir Panjal markhor bye-passes Astore, and is found in Baltistan, while in Baluchistan the heads of two rams were found, locked in combat to the death, one Astore the other Pir Panjal.

The name markhor is a compound of two Persian words meaning snake-eater. Most writers have treated with scepticism the idea that he lives up to his name, or that if he does so such a diet has any effect on his constitution. Burrard, for instance, does not even mention the matter, though Haughton in *Sport and Folklore in the Himalayas*, says that he met three men who told him convincing stories, had at first hand from their fathers, of having seen a markhor in the very act of trampling on and devouring a snake. Cobb supplied this story:

> 'When a markhor encounters a snake he kills it by stamping upon its head, and then devours it. The poison of the snake causes a cyst to grow in the stomach known as the zahr morah stone. This stone when applied to a snake bite wound absorbs the poison from the blood stream and the cure of the patient is rapid.
>
> 'I have had first hand experience of this.
>
> 'I obtained one such stone from a Gujar shepherd in Dir which came fresh from a markhor which he had been commissioned to shoot for me. When I enquired if he had found the stone he took it from his cap and sold it me for twenty rupees.
>
> 'Some time afterwards I was at a dinner party in Peshawar in a house where I was staying. A servant came in to say that a golden retriever puppy of mine in a shed in the stable had been bitten by a snake. With my friend, Colonel Sir Hissam-ud-Din, a well known shikari, I went to investigate. We found the puppy in great pain. I went to my room and brought a razor and the snake stone from my stud box. After shaving the neck we saw

the two fang marks. Making a small nick between them I clapped on the stone and held it in place.

'The stone stuck to the wound and soon began to draw it with a slight bubbling. In half an hour the puppy whose eye had been glassy was relieved from the pain of the poison and soon recovered from the effects of the bite.

'In the dust of the floor we could see the trail of the snake leading to a hole in the wall.'

Both ibex and markhor live in the most impossible terrain. Ibex favour the big spurs and the shady sides of small nullahs, markhor have a preference for precipitous slopes dropping abruptly from rocky cliffs. If there is a chink in the armour of self-preservation of either of them it is that the ibex, supremely confident in his powers as a climber, is apt to be careless of danger coming to him from above. The markhor is set in his habits, and will move each day to a particular patch of grazing. He may vary his route, but because of the difficulty of the ground there will be a point or points past which he must always go. The view has been expressed that for difficulty of approach the palm goes to solitary old markhor, but it is a close thing.

When shooting in Africa you miss through carelessness, and a miss does not rule out the possibility of a shot the following day or even a few hours later. In the Himalayas you miss through over-excitement or breathlessness due to the height at which you are moving, and you may not get a second chance. When the success of a long and expensive trip is measured in terms of one or perhaps two really good heads, you cannot afford to neglect the smallest detail to make sure that your shot, when you take it, hits the target.

The first golden rule laid down for shooting ammon—to stay in camp if it is a windy, gusty day—applies equally to a stalk in the mountains, but there the resemblance ends. On the downs the wind is virtually the only physical factor to be taken into account: the ground presents no obstacle to you or the animals you are after, and once you have located them the sooner you start to stalk the better.

You can begin with the proposition that both ibex and markhor are extremely hard to pick up even through glasses. When resting they blend so perfectly with their background that only the chance movement of a head may betray the fact that what you took for a rock or a bush is in fact a goat. The next point is that unless alarmed neither is likely to leave the slopes where you have found them. Through the day they will move up or down to rest or feed, but it is useless to think of a stalk till you have a pretty clear idea of what their movements are, with every consideration for the shift of wind in the morning and afternoon, and for the ground you will have to cross. To shorten a range of 400 yards as the bullet flies you may have to make a detour lasting a couple of hours.

Starting then with the day on which the shepherd you have engaged locally tells you that the animals you are looking for are to be found in a certain locality, it may take you another day's careful search with your glasses to single out the shootable heads. And it may take another two days to study their movements, and those of the protective screen of females they have around them: only then will you have the facts on which to plan the actual stalk.

There is a story in Kennion's book that illustrates how a trifling change in the wind, over which he had no control, ruined a stalk at the very last moment when success seemed certain.

> 'I found myself lying rifle in hand gazing across 150 yards of air at three big ibex lying on a dry ledge of rock opposite me. From the point of view which connects hill shooting with precipices it was quite typical ibex ground. I cannot recall a more awesome or pictorially appropriate scene. Great naked black cliffs rose out of the mist on all sides. Our heads projected over a sheer drop the bottom of which could not be seen. Opposite us, where the ibex lay, a wall of rock abutted up to dizzy heights, overhanging the chasm. The noise of loud rushing waters filled our ears, and from every crevice and gully streams flung themselves into space but, swept away by currents of air, became wreaths of smoke before they could touch the rock again.'

His shikari advised him to wait until the ibex got up, and wait he did, shivering with cold and excitement. Then just when he was least expecting it they rose simultaneously to their feet, moved along their gallery and were gone. A puff of air had warned them of his presence. He managed to get off a couple of shots but they were both misses. He never saw the animals again.

There are of course dozens of stories with happier endings, at any rate for the shikari, but there are few in which the physical effort involved is not predominant.

Cosmo Stewart tells one in the *Royal Artillery Journal* about a ten days' trip after ibex. On the last evening, as his leave was up, he had to press on alone, leaving his shikari to bring in an ibex he had just shot. He slept for a few cold and uncomfortable hours between two rocks, then

*Ibex Country*

> 'I got in after sunrise, dog tired, my face all blisters from the exposure and my hands raw. But after a hearty breakfast, a wash and a shave and half an hour's sleep, I did a stiff day on the hills with the battery. Such is the joy of youth.'

The same thread of difficulties overcome runs through most of the stories about the markhor:

> 'Of all known animals that lure the sportsmen in their pursuit, surely none affect such truly appalling ground as do the spiral horned markhor . . . We went through an acrobatic performance on one occasion which will always remain vividly impressed upon my memory. . . . We had reached a naked wall of rock in whose smooth surface scarcely a break was to be seen which might afford a foothold. . . . On either side the way was barred by chasms and I of course thought we should have to retrace our steps and try a fresh ascent. But not a bit of it! With the help of the villagers and his own extraordinary powers of adhering to the most impossible-looking surfaces Ramzan succeeded in getting to the top. The next moment I was hoisted on the shoulders of the man below, whence, the whole of my body pressed tight against the rock, I was ordered to proceed by stepping on to the same individual's hand held at arm's length above his head. Ramzan then reached down and seized me by the wrist and for the next few seconds I was hanging literally in mid-air with a drop of goodness knows how far straight below me.' (Ronaldshay)

But it was not his lucky day. Not only, when they came up with the herd, had the two large bucks disappeared, but on the way home a rock became dislodged as he was crossing a stream and he found himself waist deep in icy water. It was not until a fortnight later that he at last succeeded in shooting a markhor. His shikari who was moving ahead of him gave a low whistle.

> 'In front of us the mountain slope fell away, giving place to precipitous cliffs which dropped sheer to the bottom of a deep abyss. We crawled cautiously to the edge screened by a mass of boulders and the stems of fir trees.'

First a doe then a small buck appeared less than thirty yards away. The strain was becoming almost intolerable when hard on their tracks 'came bounding a hoary old buck with long flowing beard and great spiral horns. With a defiant toss of the head he halted in almost the identical spot. I was trembling like a child as I lay flat on my face and wormed the rifle along to get it in front of me. As I drew a fine bead on a point just behind his shoulder the feverish excitement, *mirabile dictu*, left me and when I pressed the trigger it was with an absolutely steady hand. As the smoke blew back in my face I saw a hazy vision of an animal take a wild leap into the air, give one frantic struggle as he landed on the very edge of the precipice and then vanish into the abyss below.'

They managed to scramble down after him and found that by great good luck his horns, though chipped and scratched, were not broken.

While in Astore and between expeditions, he enjoyed the hospitality of two officers of the Gilgit garrison whose mess was known locally as the Pig and Whistle. At the end of January he decided to set out on the crossing of the Burzil that so nearly ended in disaster. The time had come to say goodbye.

'I shook hands for the last time with Johnson. It was but a short time after that he met with a violent death claimed by a fate as pitiless as the grim mountains on which he met it for, experienced and intrepid mountaineer that he was, he lost his life indulging in the sport he loved so well. A leap on to a treacherous rock as he hurried down to examine a fallen markhor dislodged it from the mountain side, causing him to lose his balance, and those who lose it here are like to lose it for all eternity.'

# THE ROD

# 13. Mahseer

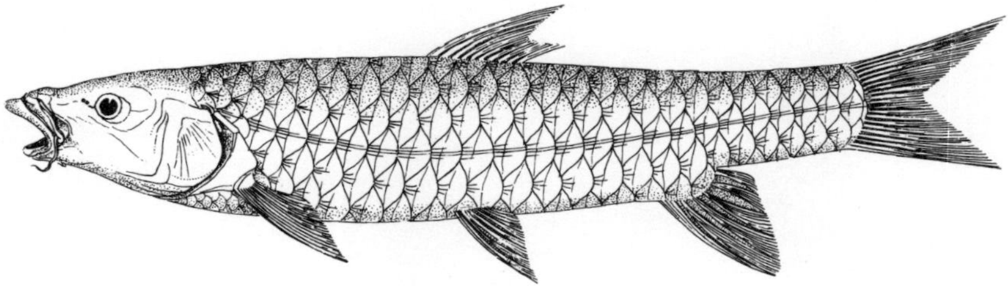

*Mahseer*

The rail-bound traveller in India, in the course of one of those interminable journeys from Bombay, saw little to give him any idea of the sport with spear, rifle and shot gun that was there for those who left the beaten track to look for it. And it was the same with the fishing. Every hundred miles or so the train would rumble cautiously over fifteen or twenty spans of a bridge that crossed a river which, during the monsoon or when the snows were melting, might roll from bank to bank in a sullen, chocolate-coloured flood. For the remaining seven or eight months it could do no more than fill a channel crossed by a single span. Either way it looked pretty unpromising, as indeed it was, for both mahseer and trout, the one indigenous the other imported, preferred the clear dashing water to be found before the rivers spilled out into the plain.

Fishing might be the main object of your leave, though even if it was, you would be wise to take a gun to deal with the odd partridge or duck you flushed along the bank. You could also combine it with other things. If a river flowed through your block in the tiger jungles of the Terai you had an agreeable sideline to while away the hours between visiting the kills in the very early morning and putting them out again at night.

There are many indigenous sporting fish in India and anyone interested in them can do no better than read *Circumventing the Mahseer and other Sporting Fish in India and Burma,* by A. StJ. Macdonald. Within the limits of this book there is room only for the mahseer.

He is found throughout the length and breadth of the subcontinent. Some of the largest fish have been caught in Madras in the Cauvery and its tributary, the Cubbany. There are mahseer in all the rivers of south India, in Baluchistan, along the North-West Frontier, in all the Himalayan streams and in Assam and Burma, where again they run very large.

He is the most sporting fish of the lot, and all things to all men. He asks no more than a stream with its source a thousand feet above sea

*Bait fishing for Mahseer*

level, to give the foaming boulder-stream rapids that he loves. The clearer, the rougher, the wilder the water the better he likes it. He is omnivorous. Small fish, beetles, grasshoppers, frogs, shrimps, snails, shells and all, and crabs as large as the palm of your hand, to be crushed in the immensely powerful teeth that lie encased in rolls of muscle at the back of his throat: teeth that can fold and crush a metal fly spoon. He also eats seeds and fruit, figs and mulberries as they drop from the tree. As he is a bottom feeder he was mostly fished for with a spoon, but he would take a fly, and in still deep pools, a paste of baked flour.

He lacked the sustained fighting power of the salmon, but for the explosive violence of the first wild rush when hooked he was in a class of his own. Macdonald says that in heavy water it can aptly be called terrifying. 'Your arms are nearly torn from their sockets and you will need all your skill and experience to keep the point of the rod up.' He concedes that of all sports pigsticking takes first place but for the rest:

> 'The whirr of the rising partridge, the swoop of the flighting duck, the call of the gorgeous monal as he hurtles through the pines, is each in its own place akin to that heart beat when the driven tiger approaches. At all such times one is spellbound by the intense enjoyment of the moment; but the instant of contact with a heavy mahseer, be he of two or three score pounds, is a thrill unsurpassed in any other sport.'

A monster of 119 lb, caught in the Cauvery by a party out for a Christmas camp in 1919, held the record for many years. She ran out all but five yards of line on the reel, then fortunately changed her mind and turned upstream. It was twenty-five minutes before they had a sight of her and the excitement was so intense that no note was made of the time of landing. At an estimate, by comparison with the sacred fish in Mysore, she may have been two hundred years old.

The best known mahseer water of all was at Tangrot where the Poonch river, which rises in the Pir Panjal, flows into the Jhelum (see map on pp. 130–31). In the spring, it is about the size of the Tweed at Coldstream, but the pools are deeper and the stream more rapid.

> 'The landscape of Tangrot is nothing to boast of. But on a winter day, when the stream is low and clear, the air still, the water rippleless, stroll to the village of Jungoo, stand on the cliff that overhangs the pool, (in the Poonch,) and gaze into the depths

> below. You will see a sight worthy of kings. Thousands of mahseer litter the bottom. There they lie like sardines in a box, marshalled in order of size. First come the giants, at the head of the pool, close to a warm water spring, the cosiest spot; half way down lie the twenty pounders; last of all come the five pounders, at the tail of the pool and on the shelving shore.'

The fame of Tangrot had spread to south India as early as 1870, as witness an article from *The Field*, dated 9th October 1869, describing a trip when two anglers in eleven days caught 87 fish totalling 1,145 lb. The largest was caught on the fourth day using a natural bait and from the last cast of the day, just as it was getting dark. After its initial run, which took out 100 yards of line, the fish tried both up and down stream before sulking for an hour. The pressure kept on him was so great that any attempt to reel in only caused the line to sink between the coils already on the reel. The only way was to draw in a few inches by hand, and then wind it up. By great perseverance he was brought to within twenty yards but no further; he then rushed off to the bottom again. By then it was quite dark. A servant was sent for a meal, and a fire was lit. About ten o'clock the screws securing the bars on the reel gave way, and it was not till 2 a.m., after two last furious runs, that he was coaxed into a shallow creek where the shikari got his hands into his gills and landed him. He weighed 52 lb. Tangrot now lies submerged beneath the waters of the new Mangla Dam.

The pursuit and capture of the really big mahseer was fair enough for those whose main interest was fishing, but for many the single handed fly rod, casting a half or one inch fly spoon, was the cream of the sport, and you could suit your tackle to the water. For a small stream, a nine foot rod and a quarter inch spoon were adequate, the next step up called for great care in the choice of rod and reel. The best you could buy was no extravagance. If a fish of four or five pounds took your spoon in heavy water the first thing you would see would be the splice between line and backing tearing away downstream, but on the same tackle you might find you were into a 25 pounder.

On a leave spent in a tiger block in the Terai, there is a memory of returning to camp early one morning after visiting the kills. None had been taken. Pausing on a bluff to look down on 150 yards of foaming rapid below, one could see a dark band extending up and downstream along the further bank. A look through the glasses showed that it consisted of hundreds of thousands of chilwa, a small fish the size of a whitebait, taking advantage of what slack water they could find to

*River near Dehra Dun*

fight their way upstream. There is nothing a mahseer likes better than a nice fresh run chilwa. It took very little time to bolt a hasty breakfast and return. The fish were quite frantic. No sooner did the spoon hit the water than it was torn away downstream. The excitement lasted nearly an hour.

And there was always something to delight the eye, even when the fish were not taking. You might be as lucky as Jim Corbett was when he watched an osprey catch a two pound fish and, holding it like a torpedo, make for its nest: but its luck was out. It was seen and chased by a Pallas fish eagle twice its size. It changed course and flew for safety among the tree tops but it was too late, and had to drop the fish which had not fallen a yard before the eagle caught it and, turning with a graceful sweep, made off downstream.

Mahseer might also be caught among far less pleasant surroundings. Baluchistan, riven by earthquakes, is a land of barren hills and stony river beds where water appears from nowhere and vanishes again a few miles lower down. If you were a Political and knew your way around you might find yourself casting a sea trout fly, a Zulu or a teal and green, over a bubbling stream bordered by willows, winding past a Pathan village through fields of grass and corn. But you might need an escort to protect you from the wild men of the hills.

> 'We each had one of the Levies as a ghillie, and two more for escort. The *daffadar* (sergeant) in charge of the post wanted us to wait until the *jemadar* (Indian Officer) came along with reinforcements but it looked safe enough, and we were all for getting under way.
>
> 'In this rather wild country the Marris are the blokes who shot up a train last year and murdered two officers, but the political agent said we should be alright if we did not go far upstream and had an escort. The river was glorious, the country the very last piece of unpleasantness that God created. You know the picture of Dante's Inferno, great red, black terraced cliffs with people having their hair pulled out? Well, it's just like that.
>
> 'I went up for two miles and from a rise saw a glorious pool about half a mile ahead. My gallant escort were not having any, and I called them cowards, so they followed. I got to my pool and posted my levies on a little rise and got to work. The first cast a fish followed the bait, the third I had him and he was away. After that my gallant escort came doubling back talking at once. I could not understand anything but "badmash" which means "a bad hat". I thought they were trying to put the wind up so I went on fishing, until I saw some local gentry coming down the stream. They looked all right, no more ruffianly than usual, but then I saw they were carrying rifles which is not allowed round Quetta. I can't say I felt very brave. I hoped there was no law against rifles in that part of the country, and as I could not very well run away I went on fishing and missed two good rises.
>
> 'While the men were still 200 yards away there was a great clatter round the bend of the nullah downstream and the levy jemadar cantered up with a section looking like comic opera bandits, going quite hard over the river bed. Torrents of Pushtu poured over me of which I collected only "badmashes" and something concerning obeying the orders of the political sahib. Anyway I gathered I had strayed from the fold and we went downstream, the jemadar and his host carrying out a gallant rearguard action against the local gentry.' (*The Field*)

In many stations there was fishing to be had more or less on your doorstep. From Rawalpindi you had only to drive out a few miles along the road to Peshawar to where a branch took off to Abbottabad.

There you found a lovely stream in a wide stony bed. One bank was lined with mulberry trees and when the fruit was ripe there was good sport to be had dapping.

'*Ek tut, ek machhli*', said the shikari. ('One mulberry, one fish.')

It needed in fact a nice co-ordination of hand and eye to strike and hook the fish before he ate the fruit. And fly fishing had been going on there since 1876.

> 'Next morning I was at the waterside before five o'clock. Looking down stream I could see a succession of long sparkling runs terminating in large pools whose waters glistened and flashed in the rays of the morning sun. The scenery around was very beautiful. Here and there clumps of small tropical trees fringed the banks while every mile or two a piece of rising ground had been selected as the site of a picturesque native village.
>
> 'From time to time a file of native women in bright coloured garments might be seen on their way to the river to fill the huge earthenware pots which they balanced on their graceful heads without an effort, while at each step the silver circlets which they wear on their comely brown limbs jangled in unison.
>
> 'I had arranged my tackle overnight and now commenced operations with three flies, two black and one gray dun. The mahseer were taking freely and I hardly made a cast without rising one. Though they were not very large it was very pretty fishing, the clear water and bright sun making every pebble visible, while I could see each fish that came at the fly and the bright flash of its side as it broke the surface of the water. I had removed the check from my reel before commencing as I had found the day before that it worked too stiffly to be safe with fine tackle, and I let every fish have as much line as it wanted to, holding it tight when its first efforts were exhausted.
>
> 'By about eight o'clock the sun was becoming very powerful and notwithstanding that I wore an enormous solar topee, a quilted pad on the back to protect the spine, and a cummerbund around my waist I was beginning to feel that its effects were disagreeable.' (*The Field*)

He would have been more comfortable if he had worn fewer clothes.

# 14. Trout

*Kashmir Trout flies*

The trout was imported into India; he cannot live in the temperature to which the water rises at heights below 5,000 feet. Nostalgia, no doubt, played a large part in inspiring the first attempts at stocking the streams in Kashmir and in the hills behind the south-western seaboard. To the planters and those who had retired to live there it seemed a shame that such tempting pools and runs should hold nothing better than small mahseer, or churoo and chush, the indigenous fish of Kashmir, which did not always take a fly, never fought with the same spirit as a trout, and above all, were not really very good to eat.

By 1901, after a couple of false starts, two brothers called Mitchell, who worked for a timber firm in Kashmir, had succeeded in hatching out ova imported frozen from Scotland. After some further vicissitudes—in 1903 a disastrous flood swept through the stockpools—the trout was firmly established and began to breed in the hatcheries that were set up. Soon after this, attempts were made to introduce them into the rivers of the Nilgiris. So far south, there are no snow fed streams and it was found that although ova of the brown trout would hatch out, the fish would not breed, so experiments were made with rainbow, also imported from Scotland. The first consignment arrived in 1906 and the tank in which they travelled was carried in a bullock cart up the road from the main line station on the plains. The trout hatched out but were found to have a kink in the spine. Next year the same thing happened. After much deliberation it was suggested that the trouble was due to the peculiar jolting, swaying motion of the bullock cart as it wound its way up the mountain. In 1908 the tank was taken up in one of the first motor cars to use the road. Driven with extreme care, the consignment arrived in perfect condition and the rainbow has thrived there ever since.

Ova from the Kashmir hatcheries were taken to stock rivers in other parts of north-west India. On the initiative of political officers in the Frontier Province, trout were introduced into several out-of-the-way places, notably to Gilgit, and from there to Chitral where the fry were transported in drums with perforations to permit aeration. They were periodically immersed in river water as they were carried on a journey of over 100 miles by relays of porters. They flourished everywhere and the record fish caught in Gilgit was twenty-five inches long and weighed over ten pounds.

These waters were not open to the ordinary fisherman, but there was one river outside Kashmir which became very well known. This was the Beas as it flowed through Kulu, where a colony of retired British army officers and civilians had settled; mostly to grow apples. They imported ova in 1909 and between the wars, Kulu was a well favoured resort of those who lacked the time or the money to go to Kashmir.

> 'From under a large boulder 13,050 feet above sea level among snow clad peaks springs the Beas, one of the principal affluents of the Sutlej. For the first five miles of its course it drops in one giddy cascade after another, a fall of 7,000 feet, gathering to itself in its mad downward rush the waters of other streams which bring down such abundant contribution from the melting glaciers that the main stream soon becomes a deep, unfordable torrent. After this first wild plunge the river steadies on its course and flows for sixty miles through the beautiful and fertile valley of Kulu.
>
> 'The Beas is quite unlike any river to be found in the British Isles. It is not a series of pools broken by falls and runs, it is a continuous chain of small falls uninterrupted by pools. It carries a huge volume of water and the current of the main stream must often reach a speed of fifteen miles an hour.
>
> 'It is too fast to contain fish who even when hooked will seldom venture into it. The fish lie close to the banks, eddies and backwaters formed by the numerous rocks that check the stream, and a good trout is often found close behind some submerged boulder on the edge of the main flow. The water is cold, as it is mainly derived from melting snow and ice, and the trout are as firm and fit as any fresh run salmon, and fight as vigorously.
>
> 'When hooked they usually dash downstream tumbling with the rushing water over one or two cascades. The angler must follow scrambling and cursing, with cut elbows and broken knees, to decide the issue in a final bout in the few square yards

of a moderately still backwater. A well liked fly is the Coachman. At times when there is no rise to a fly, fish may be caught on a fly spoon, and there is yet another method, the surest of all. Come close and let me whisper it, lest some purist should hear: it is a good fat worm.' (*The Field*)

Crossing the Pir Panjal, with the hot and dusty plains of India behind them, the Mogul emperors may well have claimed that in Kashmir they had discovered a paradise on earth. As was their wont, when they found a likely stream, they set about adorning it with terraced gardens, planted shade giving trees, and built platforms where they might sit with their court and listen to the music of the waters. But wherever he went, the fisherman would have a background of beauty that owed nothing to the hand of man: a carpet of wild flowers, dragon flies, swallowtail and tortoiseshell butterflies, paradise flycatchers, jackdaws, herons, golden orioles, kingfishers and, most beautiful of all, the blue jay which nests in holes in the high banks. He might see a black bear finishing his morning meal, or hear the challenge of the stag as he roared in the forests above the valley. He had every sort of water to choose from; a foaming torrent breaking into a long, deep pool, or a rush-lined waters-meet which in England would hold a 30 lb. salmon. If he took the road to Baltistan he came to the Kishenganga and its tributary the Burdwan, a typical dry fly stream where on tiny flies and fine gut he might catch a three pounder in the still clear water. For the even more energetic, who were prepared to camp at 12,000 feet, there was a choice of five lakes to fish in at Gangabal, high above the road to the Zoji La.

At Achabal, one of the earliest streams to be stocked, there is an old Mogul garden, shaded by chenar and stately poplar trees and surrounded by orchards of apples, pears and peaches. From the base of the perpendicular dark rocks that form one end of the garden, water wells up from deep cool springs into ice cold pools. It is led off into canals but one natural branch flows outside the garden to form a deep pool where there is a low island and a weeping willow, a lurking place for trout and a ready perch for kingfishers who can dive from where they sit. It was in the Achabal near the garden that Haughton at last caught a trout that had eluded him for a couple of days.

'As the sun dips behind the distant Pir Panjal and the doves come flocking down for their evening drink I change my flies to a coachman and a most tempting looking silver and white Hardy's lure. Crawling down to the bank and crouching there I cast with all the skill I can muster, but except for a slight ripple I am no nearer catching him than I was yesterday. There is only one thing to be done and there is just enough light from the sunset glow to do it. The cast I have been using is removed and a very fine one that I have ready is put on in its place. At the end of it is a small silver sedge. It is nearly dark but the pale twinkling stars in the east and the deep orange glow that still tints the western horizon gives sufficient light to see the little white fly I am using as it comes floating downstream. Swish—swish, sings the line above my head, the bats flutter at the waving rod, and the carefully tied sedge is put over him—and he has it. With a gentle suck he took it, but now that he is hooked there is no gentleness in his behaviour. Out he comes with a jump, then is off up the pool like a flash.

'It is my turn to be gentle for it is the finest of casts I am using. In the fast deep water he sulks for a while, but a little extra pressure moves him and he comes tearing down stream again almost to the place where he was hooked. Here he bores down and I can feel him shaking his head and jagging the line with savage and alarming jerks. I manage to keep him out of a patch of reeds, and now he is tiring a little, and I can see his back rolling out of the water, porpoise fashion. But he has plenty of fight in him and it is another good five minutes before the sharp-eyed Kashmiri boy slips the net under him and hoists him ashore in the gathering darkness.

'Three and a half pounds he proves to be, and although I am very wet and it is a long walk home in the dark, the chirp of the crickets, and the croak of the frogs, and even the harsh cry of the heron, sound as the sweetest music in my ears.'

As you moved around in Kashmir you might come across some queer fish on the bank as well as in the water. Alban Wilson in *Trout Fishing in Kashmir*, recalls meeting a nawab, a wealthy Mohammedan landowner.

'He was quite successful, which was rather surprising, for his flies were tied by his boatman and were anything but works of art. Moreover he was followed along the bank by a retinue of six or seven servants of all sorts, who never made the least effort to keep out of sight.'

Having no English himself, he entrusted the task of completing the game register to his secretary who wrote that the fishes 'were intolerably scanty', attributing the scarcity to the quite nominal punishments handed out to poachers. The first and largest fish he caught had weighed over four pounds and he was clearly disappointed that such luck did not last. Wilson met him again on the Burdwan where he was finding things more to his liking.

> 'Every day I have been catching four fishes, but if otherwise the rules I might have caught more than a dozen. The game is not interesting on the whole, if simply small ones are caught, simply for belly purposes, but it is really very amusing to catch big ones and enjoy their silly frisks.'

# THE GUN

# 15. Snipe, Geese and Duck

*Bar-headed Goose*

It was all very well in the years of plenty for the Old Shikari to pour scorn on his thistle-whipping friends who had not discovered the joys of shooting with the grooved barrel; tiger, panther, bear, boar and sambhur roamed on his very doorstep. And if anything was wanted for the pot small game was there in profusion. Pester records an evening when 'the dinner table abounded with the game we had killed. On one dish were twelve of the largest snipe I ever saw. In claret we did justice to this ample fare and parted at a late hour.'

By the 1900s it was a different story. Big game had withdrawn to the jungles. There were a few stations in the United or Central Provinces where you might still hope to shoot a panther or even a tiger on ten days' leave, but elsewhere, taking it all round the year, for the weekend outing there was only bird shooting to be had. If you were lucky enough to be able to go after chukor on the Frontier or in Baluchistan, or snipe or duck on one of the enormous stretches of marsh and water to be found near the big rivers, you would have sport as good or better than anything you would find in the United Kingdom. But right down to the end of the time covered by this book there was hardly a station in India where you could not go out with another gun before dawn on Sunday, or to sleep a Saturday night under the stars, and come back with something to show for it; maybe no more than a few brace. But it was the very stuff of life: informal, unambitious, you had to work hard for what you got, and you never knew just what you might bring home. There were places where you might pick up a mixed bag in the literal sense of the word, but generally it would be duck and snipe; or the land birds, partridge, peacock, sandgrouse and quail.

Snipe and duck started to arrive in India from their breeding grounds in Kashmir and beyond at the very end of August, and set off on the return journey about the middle of March. Between those dates they penetrated to every corner of the country, though the times and the species to be found varied a good deal from place to place. The snipe in India was an easier bird to hit than the same bird in the British Isles. He did not get up with quite the same explosive suddenness, nor jink and fly so vigorously; but the conditions under which you shot him in India were vastly more trying. Discussing snipe shooting in *Sport in Bengal* Baker refers to 'its evil reputation as unwholesome and health-destroying', and although he maintains that there should be no serious consequences if proper precautions are taken, he admits that 'it is excessively fatiguing, and those who follow it in the months of September and October must, as a matter of necessity, be prepared to sustain the burning rays of the sun on their heads and bodies, while their feet are chilled in the mud and water of the swamps and rice fields.' Another author, writing of the years 1790–1819, declares that snipe, assisted by spirits and water, were far more dangerous enemies of the young officer than Mogul or Mahratta. 'I could enumerate at least a hundred of my acquaintances who have sacrificed the most vigorous health to this very destructive sport', although they were in no way ignorant of the fact that it was 'destroying them by inches'.

The climate in northern India was less trying. All the same the man who went out after snipe had to be prepared to plod all day shin deep through evil smelling bog, a punishing form of exercise and a searching test of physical fitness.

It paid to study the bird's habits. He was elusive to locate, particularly when migrating; here today on a likely patch of ground, but gone tomorrow and back the day after: capricious too in his choice of feeding grounds, plentiful on one side of the road, none on the other. There were two main species of snipe, the pintail and the fantail, or common snipe. Except for a variation in the structure of the bill there was not to the casual eye a lot of difference between the two, but the distribution varied, as did their feeding habits. The pintail was virtually unknown west of the river Jumna or north of the United Provinces, but he was the more common of the two in south India. In Bengal they were about equal.

Baker gave instances of a single gun in Bengal shooting over fifty brace in a day, and right up to 1947 the countryside north of Calcutta was well known for its snipe shooting, but Hume records his opinion that bags in the United Provinces were even larger.

It is fitting at this point to pay tribute to Hume and the three-volume work he wrote in collaboration with Marshall, *The Game Birds of India, Burmah and Ceylon.* The text, which is meticulously accurate down to the smallest detail, is the work of Hume, who was an Indian civil servant, and represented years of personal observation in the field, supplemented by correspondence with naturalists all over the sub-continent. It was the consuming hobby of his leisure hours, and in his introduction he is unnecessarily modest in regretting that the text lacks the final polish he would have liked to give. The book was printed in India. Marshall spent a whole year in England at the time of publication in 1880, concerning himself with the production of the 150-odd coloured plates that adorn the work. He served a hard master in Hume who, if he was less than satisfied with a plate, made no bones at all about saying so. One wonders what the luckless artists thought about it. The man who drew the plates of the pintail and fantail snipe was only one to incur his displeasure. His picture of the pintail was 'not good' and 'would not help anyone materially in distinguishing between the two'. The picture of the bird flying away was 'purely an effort of the artist's imagination'. That of the fantail 'might be worse, and with name clearly written below it most people will be able to make out what it is supposed to represent'.

Hume explains the appearance of his work, though lacking its final polish, on the grounds that such a book was badly needed. It was lucky that it appeared at all. In an addendum slip to the first volume he forecasts a second and revised edition and invites corrections and suggestions, but it never materialised. Soon after publication he came to hold religious beliefs that forbade the taking of life and, feeling that he could not be responsible for a work which encouraged anyone to shoot birds, he took steps to withdraw and destroy all unsold copies. Those which survive are worth their weight in silver.

Some forty years later, his work was ably supplemented by a number of articles, remarkable for the same high standard of accuracy, contributed by E. C. Stuart Baker to the *Journal of the Bombay Natural History Society*, and published by them as bound volumes under the title *The Game Birds of India, Burma and Ceylon*. The illustrations in colour do full justice to the text.

To return to the snipe, you could escape the toil and sweat of walking up by having the birds driven over you, but because of their wayward flight and the nature of the ground on which they lived this was seldom possible. There was a well-known shoot at Chingleput in Madras, where scrub covered spurs ran down between the rice fields in which the snipe fed. When the sun got too hot they withdrew to the shade. Beaters working along the top of the spurs then drove them over guns posted along the edge of the fields. There was also one place in Kashmir where shallow waterways ran through patches of almost liquid swamp in which the reeds grew three or four feet high. The guns were poled in their shikaras, the local boat, to a patch of clear water. The beaters wore a large circular shoe made of cane and wood woven crosswise, on the principle of a snowshoe, on which they were able to walk across mud and weeds. Each carried a long pole. Sitting down it was hard to swing your gun and the crank-sided boat made it no easier, for if not well balanced, you had a chance of falling overboard. It was terribly difficult to hit those driven snipe. Showing up clearly enough against the limpid blue sky, they came down-wind like leaves in an autumn gale.

A minor hazard was that it was not unknown for the villagers to moor, somewhere in the zone of fire, a shikara containing an aged crone, past other useful work, in the hope that she would be hit by a stray shot. If the plan came off she set up a howl calculated to soften a heart of stone, though it ceased abruptly on the production of blood money, satisfied at the rate of a rupee a pellet.

There were two varieties of geese, the grey lag, the bird that is common all over Europe, and the bar-headed, which was found only in India and Burma where it outnumbered the grey lag by five to one. They were late arrivals, not reaching northern India till late October, and their habits and the method of shooting were very much the same. They were night feeders and did great damage to young crops. They spent the day on sandbanks in the nearest river. Hume notes:

> 'I do not know a more beautiful sight than the sudden and rapid descent of a large flock from high in the air to some sandbank. They come along in sober state, circle round decorously once or twice then suddenly, as though all hands had been piped to skylark, down they come with incredible rapidity, twisting

and turning with an ease and grace for which no one could at other times have given them credit.'

They might be shot by flighting or by stalking, on land or water. On land they were as worthy an object of a stalk as any black buck, but they were very wary and would test all your skill and cunning. A naturalist by name Prjevalski claimed that if he saw a pair of geese flying he could attract their curiosity enough to bring them down within gunshot by lying down and waving his hat at them. There is no evidence that anyone else found this method successful.

By water Hume favoured a punt gun, but this weapon was going out of fashion at the time he wrote his book. He describes how he used to float downstream:

> 'I float luxuriously over the glittering water fanned by the fresh cool breeze, always blowing along the valleys of our larger rivers. Around me are all my little luxuries; in my lips the peaceful pipe—guns of various sizes arranged orderly at hand. Now an old Pea Fowl or a Ravine Deer, an Otter, a crocodile or a big Turtle on the banks, offers a fascinating if difficult rifle shot; now a little swampy bend certain to harbour a few snipe, or a tempting gram patch just under the cliffs, a sure find for two or three brace of grey partridges, invite one to land for a few moments. Ever and anon a flock of cranes affords scope for careful circumventing, and whenever nothing else appears there is always a flock of geese to work judiciously.'

There were others who regarded it as a waste of time and shot to try to shoot geese by day and favoured flighting. The birds would leave their feeding grounds at first light, as soon as the villagers were on the move, and could be intercepted as they made for the river. Or, provided you could locate their feeding grounds, and the local inhabitants were usually only too willing to help, the evening was a better time, with the chance that there would be duck on the move also.

The well-travelled sportsman who has shot duck in the United States, Canada or Egypt, generally stakes a claim for this or that country as providing the best shooting in the world; whatever their merits, India, at any rate up to the end of last century, would have come very high on the list. Hume and Marshall describe about twenty-five varieties of duck and teal that regularly visited India, Burma and Ceylon, each with its own likes and dislikes in the matter of food and feeding grounds that dictated its choice of river, lake or swamp on which to spend the winter, and decided the locality in which they were most plentiful. Teal, gadwall, mallard, widgeon, pintail and red-crested pochard, in a rough order of their arrival, were the best known; all fine sporting birds, each, according to your personal preference, a candidate for the honour of favourite at the dinner table.

A well known shot, one Colonel Tickell, who lived a hundred years ago wrote, 'As welcome as on the mountains the feet of him who bringeth glad tidings are the first flights of the Water Fowl, which announce to the nearly exhausted European the approach of the delicious cold weather of India.' And when the water fowl did arrive one of the great attractions was the immense variety of sport they afforded. You might be on a large jheel where you needed boats and half a dozen guns, or on a small patch of mud and water, where with a friend you would have a capital morning's sport, shooting from the bank or wading through the shallows. If you knew a likely spot you could go in for flighting, taking the birds as they left the water to feed by night in the fields. Sport would last no more than an hour, but if there was a moon to help a couple of guns could pick up fifteen or twenty brace of teal and duck.

No two shoots were the same but the secret of success was a knowledge of the habits of the species you were dealing with and a study of the water you were shooting over. The duck was a wild, free-flying bird which fell to the man who held his gun straight.

In Volume LXV of the *Journal of the United Service Institution of India*, there is an article on duck shooting by Brigadier E. J. Ross. He was a magnificent shot with rifle, pistol and shotgun, and a veritable mine of down-to-earth information as to how to set about shooting pretty well everything that ran or flew. He leaves you in no doubt that if you aspire to be a successful duck shot you must expect to work very hard, and not mind how wet and how dirty you get. You must find the line of flight of the birds, twenty yards one way or the other may make all the difference, and you must be prepared to shoot sitting, lying or in any cramped position. Concealment is all important. Duck are exceptionally keen-sighted and if they see a 'florid and expectant face' sticking up above a tuft of grass they will swerve away before they come within gun shot. He advises you to buy one of the large copper bowls in which sweetmeat sellers in the bazaar boil their milk. This will hold 300 cartridges and will keep them, and your pipe, tobacco and matches, dry as you make your way waist deep through the water. Practical down to the smallest detail, he warns you that you may find 'that your wife will pinch it

Season 1909 – 10 Gun C. O. Lowsley Jacobabad

| Date. | Ground. | Snipe. | Teal. | Duck. | Quail. | Partridge | Sandgrouse | Pigeon. | Hare. | Jungle Fowl. | Various. | | | Total. |
|---|---|---|---|---|---|---|---|---|---|---|---|---|---|---|
| '09 | | | | | | | | | | | | | | |
| Brought | forward | 39 | - | 94 | 40 | 116 | - | 53 | 4 | - | - | | | 346 |
| Dec^r 10^th | Nurwah Mouth | - | - | - | 4 | 15 | - | - | - | - | - | | | 19 |
| " 11^th | " " | - | - | - | 1 | 29 | - | - | 1 | - | - | | | 31 |
| " 15^th | " " | - | - | - | 3 | 14 | - | - | - | - | - | | | 17 |
| " 25^th | Hingorni | 72 | - | - | - | - | - | - | - | - | - | | | 72 |
| " 26 | Tregura | - | - | 52 | - | - | - | - | - | - | - | | | 52 |
| " 27^th | Brahui | 40 | - | 6 | - | - | - | - | - | - | 1 | Curlew | | 47 |
| " 28^th | Sindri | - | - | - | 15 | 5 | - | - | - | - | - | | | 20 |
| " 29^th | Hingorni | 75 | - | - | - | - | - | - | - | - | - | | | 75 |
| " 30^th | Tregura | - | - | 37 | - | - | - | - | - | - | - | | | 37 |
| | Totals | 226 | - | 189 | 63 | 179 | - | 53 | 5 | - | 1 | | | 716 |

Christmas Shoot

as a bowl in which to keep her beastly flowers'. Should this happen you are advised to retaliate by borrowing the baby's bath.

Never did the social round in cantonments seem so hollow, the festivities at the club so pointlessly alcoholic, as at Christmas. It was a time when every right-minded man took a few days' leave and headed for the open air. Shooting was almost invariably the background, and if there was duck shooting to be had you could wish for nothing better: not too strenuous, and with the certainty of good sport.

The last 200–300 miles of the river Indus are flanked by enormous tracts of marsh and shallow water where the duck and snipe came in their thousands, and the page from the game book of C. O. Lowsley of the Public Works Department who went out near Hyderabad shows what could be expected. There were ten guns in all, and their bag for the week totalled 635 snipe, 243 duck and 53 partridge and quail. There is an account in *The Field* of another Christmas shoot in the same part of the country, where a party of five guns and two wives were invited by the commissioner of the district.

> 'The people are very hospitably inclined, the *zemindars* (landowners) over whose ground one shoots fighting for the honour of being entertainers and making the arrangements. . . . What a sight when the first gun goes off, duck and all sorts of waterfowl rise in confusion, with countless numbers flying in every direction. They come so fast, on your left, right, overhead and at all angles that you can hardly hold your gun it becomes so hot. Just as you are about to abandon all hope of their return your coolie touches you and says, *sotto voce*, "*Ata sahib*" (they are coming), or you hear an indescribable rustling of silken feathers, the delight of sportsmen, and out of the very heavens comes a flight, followed by others. . . . At last, when it is evident they do not mean returning, the guns meet, gather up their spoil and go off round the edges of the water looking for stragglers. On counting the bag we find it amounts to 212 duck and snipe. And such duck: mallard, pintail, gadwall, tufted pochards, red crested pochards, yellow eyed pochards, marbled duck and shovellers. The bag may not seem large to those accustomed to shooting at home but the charm is combined with the surroundings and it is free to all alike. . . . Our total for the four days amounted to 1,928 duck and snipe and a few various. So ended our Christmas shoot. That night some of us left and by the following day everyone had dispersed, thanking our host for the excellent sport and, last but not least, for the

recollection it will always bring to mind, of which no one can rob us.'

If you moved in exalted circles you might get an invitation from an Indian prince to shoot on one of his preserves. Kashmir was a staging post for most of the duck that came into north-west India and the numbers to be seen on Hokra and Haigam, the two state jheels, were probably greater than anywhere else. Hokra was very lovely, and from your butt you would look over the tops of the reeds at the snow caps of the Pir Panjal: until you were reminded of the business in hand by a 'roar like the backwash of a big wave on a shingly beach' and looked down and saw the duck rising in a dark cloud from the water. But Kashmir was a long way away, and better known was the shoot arranged by the Maharajah of Bharatpur. His capital lay ninety miles south of Delhi, and each year the Viceroy and the Commander-in-Chief and other distinguished persons went down for one of these great occasions. Near the lunch enclosure, on a pedestal, stands a column on which is inscribed the names of the famous, and the bags they made. On 1st December 1902, Lord Curzon and Lord Kitchener were both there, and recorded only the modest total of 540 birds: they were perhaps too busy trying to shoot one another. On the last day of the year 1910, H.I.H. The Crown Prince of Germany with fifty guns, secured a bag of 1,378, while the record stands against the name of Lord Chelmsford in 1916, when fifty guns shot 4,206.

With your invitation, which included a list of your fellow guests, you received explicit instructions as to when shooting would start and stop. The signal for it to begin was fired from one of the old muzzle loading guns of the State artillery. You also got a blue-print on which was traced in red the route to the butt you had been allotted. The butts were built on the high banks that criss-crossed the swamps and flooded fields. On arrival you would find it furnished with a table with numbered compartments to hold cartridges loaded with different sizes of shot, pegs for hats and coats, and a chair for your lady friend, if you had one with you. To act as beaters there would be four troopers of the Household Cavalry, naked except for their loincloths. Any bird you dropped dead around your butt you could count as yours; those that fell further away went to swell the bag of guests more distinguished than you were. You would need two guns, a loader, and at least 300 cartridges, which you would expect to fire off before the excellent lunch that would be provided. It was wise to have a glove to protect your left hand from the heated barrels, and a pad to slip inside your shirt to cushion your shoulder.

If you were shooting well you might expect to get 100 birds, with perhaps a brace of geese, if they came over your butt when shooting began, and you might take away with you as many as you needed. It was a test of your ability to shoot straight but not of very much else except what Ross describes as 'the self-control called for when the myrmidons of the exalted personage in the next butt made off with the birds you had killed'.

# 16. Partridges, Pheasants and Others

*Frankolin or Black Partridge*

Hume and Marshall devote the first volume of their work to bustard, sand grouse, peafowl, pheasant and jungle fowl; and the second to partridge and quail; ninety-four birds in all, of which many are no more than variations, peculiar to Burma or Ceylon, of species well known in India. Unless you were a naturalist as well as a sportsman there were many you would never meet, but the ordinary soldier moving between stations in the north and south of the country would certainly come across the grey and the black partridge, the quail, and the jungle fowl wherever he went, the chukor and the see-see on the bare stony hills of the North-West Frontier and Baluchistan, and the snow partridge and the pheasants among the snows and pines of the lower Himalayas. Something, in fact, wherever he was stationed.

There are few works devoted exclusively to scatter-gun shooting but in books dealing with big game, or in the pages of *The Field*, there is no lack of stories recording some memorable day's sport. The difficulty is to choose between them, to single out the bird and the occasion, the highlights that seldom came the way of the ordinary man. Maharajahs or governors of provinces might have their *rukhs* where the occasional big shoot would be staged, but most bird shooting was what in this country would be called rough shooting: the birds were all wild and the bag prized for its variety as much as for its numbers. In picking out the examples that follow, credit has been given on three counts. Was the shooting difficult? Not only because of the bird's flight but because the ground he lived on made unusual demands on fitness or sureness of foot. Was there anything special about the surroundings? And did success depend on a knowledge of the birds' habits?

Starting in the north there was the chukor, very much the same as the Frenchman, the red-legged partridge. He is a remarkable bird. In India he is found from Nepal all along the Himalayas, the North-West Frontier and Baluchistan, pretty well down to the Arabian Sea. And he continues on through Afghanistan and Persia to the hills of Palestine and the rift of the Jordan Valley. He is equally at home at sea level or 16,000 feet up in Ladakh; where the noonday heat rises to 150° or drops to zero during the night; in a rainfall of 100 inches a year, or where it hardly rains at all.

In October he was found in coveys of ten to fifteen birds and could be walked up. A bit of a runner, it was possible to mark the birds of a covey down after they had dispersed at the first shot. He is a noisy bird, calling repeatedly in a sharp, clear tone that may be heard a mile away in the thin mountain air. He will call even when undisturbed, but

> 'when a covey has been dispersed, each individual member may be heard proclaiming his own and anxiously enquiring after all his fellow's whereabouts. The tone varies. First he says, "I'm here, I'm here." Then he asks "Who's dead? Who's dead?" And when he is informed of the untimely decease of his pet brother or favourite sister, or perhaps his eldest son and heir, he responds "Oh, lor, Oh, lor," in quite a mournful tone.'

On the Frontier of course he speaks Pushtu, and it is there, and in Baluchistan, that he provides the finest sport. A morning on the ridges and valleys of a long hillside will test the endurance of the fittest, and you need the agility of a cat to change your feet on the shifting stones to take the bird that gets up out of a bush under your elbow and swings downhill away behind your right shoulder.

'As we top the next rise a grey shadow slips over the ridge into the re-entrant beyond. Hurrying forward we stand at the top while the coolies roll stones down the slope. On the far side a chukor gets up and we give him both barrels, only to find he is out of range. And so it goes on. Sometimes they will wait on the ridge top for you, and if you have regained your breath before gaining the last few feet you will probably get a reasonable shot. The next time, perhaps, they will have run down on to the downward slope and then if you can remember not to take the first bird to rise, which is sure to be just out of shot, you will find the covey near you and see a brace crash on to the rocks below. But those are not the only shots you will get.' (*The Field*)

The cream of chukor shooting is the driven bird. If beaten out of the clumps of scrub at the head of the nullah they come down like rockets, with an almost imperceptible tilt of the wings that develops a swerve which will defeat you however smoothly you swing your gun. The story in *The Field* continues:

'Suddenly there will be a cry of "Mark, sahib!" and down the hill from the top guns swings a covey. There are few birds, driven grouse in a gale of wind included, to give a better shot than chukor coming off the tops. And here is no comfortable butt to stand in. Even as you turn a stone gives way under you, and you are on your knees trying to pull your muzzle in front of them.'

Sport of all kinds was one of the compensations for the garrison in Chitral who, except for the occasional post runner fighting his way through the winter snow drifts, were cut off from India for five months in the year.

'The Chitrali beaters encircle the head of the valley high above the guns, and descend systematically rousing the birds, since they beat similarly in their own favourite sport of hawking. The drive is very thoroughly carried out and few birds break back. During the drive one requires a hundred eyes and a grim determination to stick to one's original choice. A pack swings into view away above one on the hillside and skirts contouring towards one. Gently you swing round on your shooting stick, positioning yourself for the covey. Swish, swish, and away over your left shoulder whooshes another lot you had not spotted and drops, wings set, at sixty miles an hour down the hillside. The temptation to speed their retreat is great, but if you do, the original pack will probably serve you the same trick and so *ad infinitem.*' (*The Field*)

The chukor has a little cousin, the see-see, not unlike him in appearance, less than half his weight, and with colouring more subdued to camouflage him among the greys and browns of the low hills that are his home in the northern Punjab and the Frontier. A great runner, you may chase him a couple of hundred yards along the hillside till, as you reach the spur that marks your immediate limit of vision, he swerves away down hill and out of sight; but as part of a mixed bag he was by no means to be despised. There is an account of such a shoot by Stuart Baker:

> 'I once knew a colonel who declared that he had shot every feather off a see-see and then it had flown away naked. This may be an exaggeration but it serves to bear out my own limited experience that he is not an easy bird to hit, and when hit is not always in the bag.'

He goes on to recall a morning in a nullah where the hills join the plain south-west of Peshawar. It was before the days when everyone had a car. He had to start before it was light to catch any sand-grouse that might come down to water in the stream.

> 'Ears tingled with the cold that brought water to the eyes, and thick boots and gloves served to keep a vestige of warmth in feet and fingers. And yet, there was a wonderful fascination in skirting the sleeping city whence came as yet no sound but the barking of a dog, the tinkling of bells from some shaggy camel drowsily shaking his head in the Kabul serai, the crowing of a cock, or the voice of the muezzin, each in his own way heralding the dawn, sharp and clear in the frosty air.'

Arrived at the nullah they lit a fire of straw and sticks to warm their hands before they began to shoot. With the shikari he followed the line of the nullah with a man above him on the hill and another out in the plain to catch the birds on the edge of the crops.

> 'We had scarce gone a hundred yards when out came a see-see from a deep water-worn fissure in the cliffs. I can see that bird

> now as he shot down the cleft towards me and then, as my gun went off, he swerved abruptly round the corner with the result that I missed him badly and plastered the cliff with shot yards behind him. . . . Occasionally a bird would cross the nullah, but generally they skimmed away following the line of the cliffs and then slipping round the corner. Or they would come over the cliff, jink, turn and swing away the moment they saw one, offering most puzzling shots in their sudden changes of direction.
>
> '. . . A couple of blue rock pigeon were added to the bag, and some duck, disturbed higher up and coming straight down the stream, gave me a beautiful shot which resulted in the death of their leader, a fine drake gadwall.
>
> '. . . A patch of scrub gave me a right and left at ordinary grey partridge but the last shot, before halting for a late breakfast, was in some ways the most satisfactory.
>
> '. . . I had been trying to beat out a couple of see-see. One flew off, the other, before disappearing, had slipped round the corner, his whole person exuding the essence of impertinence, and that was the last I ever saw of him. Just as we were giving up, a soft note made me look up in time to see two imperial sandgrouse coming straight down the nullah. They were moving at a great pace and neither showed a sign of being touched as I fired; but whilst following them ruefully with my eyes I saw one crumple up and fall stone dead 150 yards behind me.
>
> '. . . One gadwall, one sandgrouse, one grey partridge, some blue rock and nine see-see, which I had got by eleven o'clock, were the outward signs of a very pleasant morning.'

If you were shooting in Spiti, Kulu or Chamba you might meet the snow partridge. He is a bird of the mountains and seldom comes below 7,000 feet, indeed you were more likely to find him between 10,000–14,000 feet. Few have actually shot him, and he enjoyed this immunity because his favourite haunts, close up under the snow, among grey crags and hoary precipices were the haunts also of thar and burhel, and if you were after larger game you had no choice but to let the lesser go. He is a dark handsome bird, with deep red legs and a coral red beak, and a strong and rapid flight, much like that of a grouse. In comparatively unfrequented spots he affords superb sport. Hume has a description of a morning after these birds that conjures up vividly a picture of the country in which they live.

> 'Amid snowy domes and peaks glistening sharp cut against the blue sky; below, almost under one's feet, and stretching

away for miles, a sea of green forest; in front, alternate patches of close shaven, mossy turf, starred with a few Alpine blossoms, and bare slaty slabs, those in the shade still silvered by the morning's frost—all sloping at a frightful angle, and traversed by little snow runlets and long streaks of partly discoloured snow, running down tiny gorges. . . . From the depths beneath, the lowing of cattle steals upwards, mellowed by the distance and mingled with faint murmurs from the torrents below; a bee or two passes humming softly; a stone clatters down over the shale; the surging murmur of a distant avalanche creeps along the hillside, and then again a stillness as of death pervades the scene.

'Suddenly from the bare rocks in front out rings a loud whistle, and then another, and another; and again all is still. It is not good walking; and between you and the whistlers, stones and snow every now and then coming down as if preparatory to an avalanche; you have to mind your feet; it is impossible to say which is the more slippery, the stones or the moss, and a single false step would shoot you some two or three thousand feet into the birch trees below; but the whistle bursts out, not fifty yards away, with redoubled energy, echoing harshly among the crags. You push on, half sliding, to a little plateau close to where the whistles sounded; you scrutinise the purplish grey stones in front of you; you cough, raise your gun; still nothing is to be seen. But your dog's eyes, as he stands, his chain held by a hillman, shivering with excitement, are almost starting out of his head. . . . The man heaves a big stone a few yards in front of the dog's nose; *presto*, as if by one impulse, in one lump, with a clatter of a hundred partridges, up springs the covey; they rise perpendicularly for about three yards, and your first barrel rakes them, dropping three, the second catches the hindermost bird as they sweep down the hillside. . . . Before the echoes of the shot have died away, a growl, as if of anger at being disturbed, at first low, but growing louder every second floats down from the peaks above; a rolling cloud, a confused mist of snow, in which a few black specks are discernible, is coming straight down on you. You reach the birds when with a surging swish and mighty clatter, down rushes the avalanche, stray fragments of stone striking, and the skirts of the snow sweeping even the little plateau whence you fired. A near thing, but the birds have been marked down less than a quarter of a mile ahead . . . You push on recklessly over ground that, at other times, you would cross at a snail's pace, until the harsh whistle warns you again that the game is at hand. And now, if you have luck, you will get within the space of two hundred yards, from three to six as fine shots, singles and doubles, as ever gladdened the heart of sportsman. . . . A few days later, discussing some of these (cooked gypsy fashion) beside the perfumed blaze of a deodar bon-fire, the most miserable victim of *ennui* would be compelled to admit there was still something to live for.'

There are few points of similarity between shooting pheasants in the Himalayas and at a covert side in this country. The birds and their habitat are different, and so were the methods employed. With the exception of the cheer, the Indian pheasants are much more compact than the bird that is still a familiar sight in the English countryside. For beauty the palm goes perhaps to the monal.

> 'There are few sights more striking than that of a grand old cock shooting out horizontally from the hill-side just below one, glittering and flashing in the golden sunlight, a gigantic rainbow-tinted gem, and then dropping stone-like, with closed wings, into the abyss below.'

Small wonder that the artist's effort failed to meet with Hume's approval. 'The plate fails utterly to convey any adequate conception of the intensely brilliant metallic lustre of the upper plumage of the male.' He has the grace to add that 'perhaps no chromo *could* accurately reproduce this'.

The pheasants lived in dense cover at any height from 5,000 feet up to the tree line, and pheasant shooting called for something more than a firm seat on a shooting stick or in the Land-Rover waiting to wheel you to the next stand.

> 'Unless you are a man, such as my old friend Wilson was, able to walk forty or fifty miles up and down without fatigue, it is all nonsense going pheasant shooting in the Himalayas without the necessary aids and in the proper manner.
>
> 'You must have good dogs (small cockers are best), thoroughly under control, who will work exactly to command, and obey the whistle, and you must have a number of intelligent hill-men, something of sportsmen themselves, to search out the shooting grounds, and when you are shooting, *mark* the birds that get away from well chosen posts. I used to have four dogs and over a dozen men.'

You never expected to shoot a lot of birds and they might well be restricted to a single species, but here is a good story of a shoot that produced a mixed bag.

> 'We left camp just as the first streaks of dawn showed over the giant peaks, and wended our way slowly up the ridge, and were greeted at every few steps by the guttural call of the koklass pheasant or the more musical double note of the monal. An Irish setter and two field spaniels went ahead, and we had not gone half a mile before a cock koklass flushed by the dogs came down as only a koklass knows how on my side of the ridge and a barrel in his chest crumpled him up.
>
> 'As we approached the top of the spur we saw several monal feeding on the opposite slopes of the hill in the open. To get them without disturbing them we had to retrace our steps through thick scrub, cross over at a wooded point and descend a ravine on the other side on which grew a heavy forest of oak. Before we had gone twenty yards a cock monal soared over A's head and next instant he fell with a heavy thud. We had got fairly into their midst and though those we had seen on the opposite side were as far off as ever it was evident we should get all the shooting we wanted where we were. A's shot was the signal for a general rise to the accompaniment of a regular chorus of shrill whistling and the whirr of heavy wings in all directions, and two more birds were added to the bag.
>
> 'In the scrub immediately on my right I had heard the plaintive note of a tragopan and had not heard the heavy whirr of his wings, so called up my setter and put him in. As he came out the sun glinted on his crimson neck and in an instant later he fell in a crumpled heap not twenty yards from the point whence he rose.
>
> 'An ascent of a couple of thousand feet brought us to well above the limit of trees, and three thousand five hundred feet above our camp, so we called a halt for breakfast and a rest. While the kettle boiled we gloated over the beauties of nature which met the gaze in every direction. The endless and ever varying forest-clad slopes of oak and conifers, the deep ravines now almost bare of vegetation, with here and there great patches of leafless horse chestnuts, all dwindling away into the blue of the distant horizon, whilst above us towered the mighty giants clad in their mantle of glistening snow. A thin waterfall quite near us was frozen solid and stood like a pillar, reflecting rainbow tints. A flock of red-billed choughs circled below and

above us, and except for their merry call not a sound disturbed the silence.

'Very soon after breakfast we came upon the diggings of snow cock. Wing-wink-wing-wink, the dogs cocked their ears and we stopped and tried to locate the sound. A. had spotted a covey running uphill a hundred yards ahead. We decided to spread out and send the dogs up to flush them. The covey scattered and rose, half a dozen going over our heads. Our men had marked them down so we took good note of the country and decided to stay where we were, and send the men to drive them back. Our luck was in, the men did their work well, and having got beyond the birds, they climbed above them under cover of a spur and drove the whole covey back to us. A. dropped his first bird, wounded another and I was able to drop another, my second shot being a clean miss.

'We picked up A's and went off down hill to look for his second, but when still two hundred yards away we heard a shriek like the tearing of new silk, and looking up saw a pair of golden eagles dropping from the blue sky like rockets and next minute the snow cock was in the talons of one of them, and that was the last we saw of it. We sauntered on down the hill for tea in a nice secluded corner, sheltered from the cutting breeze, and were glad of what little warmth we got out of the sinking sun. We got back to camp betimes and our two coolies laid a very pleasing bag before the tent, consisting of one cock and three hen monal, a cock and a hen tragopan, three koklass, two snow cock, four snow partridges and a woodcock: a good mixed bag and a glorious day.

Strictly speaking the quail does not qualify for a mention. There was nothing special about the country he lived in and he was not a difficult bird to hit, but he was found all over India and was a great delicacy of the dinner table.

Hume gives fifteen varieties of quail. He is a migratory bird which arrives in India very early in the autumn, coming in successive waves over the Himalayas or from the west, and spreading far and wide over India. For the next four or five months a few quail might be picked up in any mixed shoot, but it was in the spring when the first crops began to ripen that they collected in vast hordes in the north-west before leaving the country. It was then that quail shoots were arranged and very large bags recorded. Hume talks of driving quail which must have given better sport, but in general you walked them up through stubble or low crops. A dog, or very well disciplined beaters, were essential, as the birds sat tight but, unlike the snipe, flew straight when they got up so that they presented no great challenge. They were quarrelsome little birds and were kept for fighting and it was common on the Frontier to see a Pathan boy carrying a quail and bouncing the bird's legs against the palm of his hand to strengthen them for the next encounter.

Another borderline case is the sandgrouse of which Hume lists eight varieties. The imperial and the common were those most generally shot. The latter was a resident, the former a migrant who disappeared when the weather warmed up in the spring, departing to breed, probably in the mountains of Persia. The sandgrouse has a liking for level, sparsely wooded and sandy ground and is widely distributed across the vast belt of desert down the left bank of the Indus. He is very fixed in his habits. Up with the dawn, he will feed for a couple of hours and must then fly in search of a drinking place. Spending no more than a couple of minutes at the water's edge, he returns to the open country where he will feed and rest till the afternoon, when again he must drink.

There were two ways of shooting them. You could go out in the middle of the day, and if you came across them they would be there in thousands, and the skill lay in stalking rather than in the shooting. If you succeeded in getting within range you could do no more than fire into the cloud of birds as they rose. Alternatively you might intercept them on their way to water, success depending on how many drinking places there might be. If there were some miles of river bank to choose from it was not easy to hit off the line of flight. Packs might consist of anything from 20–200 birds and would come so high that they would be hard to pick up. Even when you were on the lookout the first notice of their arrival would be the peculiar chuckling, a far-reaching double call, which they continually utter while in flight.

In districts where you might expect to find them it was always worth keeping your ears open for that far away music but there were few places, perhaps only one, where sandgrouse were the sole object of the shoot. This was in Bikanir, 250 miles west of Delhi, where the Maharajah's parties were famous. The essence of the matter was that for 48 hours beforehand all watering places were policed, and the birds prevented from drinking, except at the one where the shoot was to take place. At sunrise the birds would arrive in their thousands and for a hectic hour or two sport was fast and furious.

> 'There will probably be many who will imagine from the size of the bag that the imperial is an easy bird to bring down: do not

let me encourage any such an idea. The leading bird of a pack approaching water often gives the gun a comparatively easy shot but to make sure of securing another grouse with the second barrel taxed the skill of the best shot among us. At the first report of a gun the grouse twist and turn with almost incredible swiftness and become in my humble opinion far harder to stop than driven grouse on a Scotch or Yorkshire moor. Swinging high down the line pack after pack which looked as though they must be exterminated escaped with but little loss.' (*The Field*)

Fair enough for the couple of hours that it lasted, but for variety and charm of surroundings these occasions did not stand up to comparison with a duck shoot on the state jheels in Kashmir or Bharatpur.

Apart from the duck and the snipe, it was the two partridges, the grey and the black, that up and down the country, month in, month out, made up the greater part of the entries in the game book. The grey prefers dry, warm ground, interspersed with scrub and low grass jungle in the neighbourhood of cultivation, and as these conditions are universally found, so is the grey common over most of India. He does not rate very highly as a game bird, as he is an inveterate runner and hard to flush, but when he rises it is with the true partridge whirr, and he flies strongly and swiftly. He is fond of the outskirts of villages and has a reputation as a dirty feeder. One writer claims that he saw a covey run out of the carcase of a camel. He is terribly pugnacious, and among Mohammedans was kept as a fighting bird.

Whatever his shortcomings he has a clear, ringing, inspiriting call; *ka, ka, kateetur, kateetur, teetur* being the vernacular name for the bird. Once heard it can never be forgotten:

'In Upper India these piercing notes are so inseparably connected with our happy camp life and all its delights, that even in the dismal lanes of Calcutta the cry of a caged bird sends a thrill through one.

'In the morning, when the grass and the thickets are spangled with dew, and the welcome sun drives away the chilling fog of an Indian winter's night, the cheerful sounds are heard all over the awakening country—sounds redolent of old associations. The aroused camp striking its tents, the grateful cup of coffee by the log fire, the fragrant Manilla, the hum of the gathering column, the early march along the wild road.'

*Elephant retrieving Partridge*

The black partridge is found north of a line running east and west through Karachi; south of that his place is taken by the painted partridge. There is not a lot of difference between them, the hens being very much alike. They are beautiful speckled birds, owing nothing to exotic colouring or metallic sheen. The black favours well watered tracts with plenty of cover, while the painted is more likely to be found in the same country as the grey. Within their respective areas both birds were common. They rise well and fly strongly, and a beat through sugar cane or high crops would give splendid sport.

Grey and black partridge were very much the birds of the mixed jungle shoot. Although it was sport to be enjoyed only by those lucky enough to number among their friends those who had elephants at their disposal, shooting from the back of a well-trained animal in the grasslands of a Terai jungle had a charm all its own. Excitement and interest never flagged and, apart from the variety, a good bag might include as many as eighteen different birds and animals, ranging from quail and snipe to deer and panther. One saw a multitude of birds, 'red and gold minivets, golden orioles, rose-headed parakeets, golden-backed woodpeckers' flashing in the sun against a background of the Himalayan snows. It was a sight denied to the earthbound mortal who slogged through the grass on foot.

The air was crisp and sweet with the early morning smells of the jungle and went to the head of man and bird alike. Both were a bit too quick off the mark. Around you was a waving sea of silvery-feathered grass in which you might catch an occasional glimpse of the line of beaters, or of the other guns like moving islands on their elephants. From right under your elephant's trunk a partridge would get up, perpendicularly, until he was a yard above the grass, and then skim away in straight, strong flight. Quail, jungle fowl, peafowl, deer, you never knew what would come next, though in Hume's opinion these were but 'kickshaws, incidental and intrinsic delicacies'. The real *pieces de resistance* were the black partridge. If you were used to howdah shooting, and it was an art that not everyone mastered, the birds were not particularly hard to hit. One Colonel Congreve is credited with shooting six running with ball from a smooth bore gun.

Moreover, there was always the chance of something completely unexpected. Corbett describes one such occasion on a day when a line of fourteen elephants, with nine guns, had on their first beat picked up five peafowl, three red jungle fowl, ten black partridge, four grey partridge, two bush quail and three hare. He halted the line and swung to face the Himalayas. Hanging in the sky directly in front of them was a brilliantly lit white cloud that 'looked solid enough for angels to dance on'. They had gone about a mile, collecting thirty more birds and a panther, when a ground owl got up, flew straight for about fifty yards, then suddenly started to gain height by flying round and round in short circles. The reason became apparent when a peregrine falcon, flying at great speed, came out of the trees to the left. A contest between the two birds began, the owl spiralling upwards with rapid wing-beats, the falcon circling on wide-spread wings trying to get above his quarry. The line halted, for no one had eyes for anything else. The two birds had reached a height of perhaps a thousand feet when the owl, still circling, started to move away towards the cloud. It was clear what it was trying to do, and 'one could imagine the angels suspending their dance and urging it to make one last effort to reach the shelter of their cloud'. Suddenly from the ground only one bird was to be seen. The owl had made it, and the falcon in one long, graceful glide came back to the tree from which he had started.

> 'The reactions of human beings to any particular event are unpredictable. Fifty-four birds and four animals had been shot that morning, and many more missed, without a qualm or the batting of an eyelid. And now guns, spectators and *mahouts* were unreservedly rejoicing that a ground owl had escaped the talons of a peregrine falcon.'

The jungle fowl is a true denizen of the jungle, favouring tracts that bordered on scattered cultivation and remained well watered through the year. The red jungle fowl lives in north India, the grey in the south. The former very much resembles the domestic bantam with a shorter, sharper crow. If you did not wish to disturb any larger game you might be after it might be stalked and shot for the pot with a ·22 rifle. A very wary, alert bird, it was adept at dodging and running through the undergrowth, but it was possible to drive it, and it then flew at a great pace and gave good shooting. It was as well to remember when taking part in these occasions that a beat laid on for jungle fowl might hold larger game. Hume has a story of meeting four bears, one of which charged him, and advises the novice always to have a rifle in trustworthy hands close behind him.

A story in the *Royal Artillery Journal* has an even more unusual ending. The shoot was in the hands of Brigadier Ross, who was then commanding his battalion in Dehra Dun, the beaters being recruits from the regiment. All went well on the first day and the bag amounted to 25 brace of jungle fowl and a brace of pheasants. Next day, at the start of the second beat of the morning there was suddenly a hush, a complete absence of the more easily startled game which usually heads the rush away from the beaters. The reason became clear when a tigress came out. She was shot by one of the guns. No tigers had been seen in that locality for several years, but she was in season and had attracted, to compete for her favours, two tigers. One was shot the next day, and the day after the other was wounded and finally shot by Ross himself after a follow up arranged with all the skill of which he was a master.

Soon after this one of the young Gurkhas was charged by a sambhur and suffered a face wound, and a motor ambulance was sent out from Dehra Dun to pick him up. Ross, practical as always, was not the man to let slip the chance of sending his tiger back to cantonments, and the bloodstained body was loaded in at the back with the casualty.

Sub-assistant surgeons of the Indian Medical Service were a peaceable and law abiding class, and the man who opened the ambulance door when it reached the hospital was horrified at such a flagrant breach of the regulations. He would have none of it and, after removing the Gurkha, ordered the vehicle off to the colonel's bungalow. Among his other good qualities the Gurkha has a well-developed sense of humour, and the story goes that when a weary Ross got home late that evening, he found that he had to share a room for the night with the body of his late enemy. But he was not the man to let that disturb his slumbers.

# 17. Princes and Rich Men

*Household cavalry*

The princes of the independent states of India were in their heyday, a remarkable body of men. Judged by Western standards they were eccentric, extravagant and despotic; in their own eyes and in the eyes of those they ruled, they did no more than tread the paths worn by the feet of a long line of ancestors.

Lavish hospitality was a point of honour, a traditional way of expressing it was in the field of sport. There was no parliament to question what they spent; their word was law and no one dreamt of querying it. Their household troops, by regiments and battalions, turned out to act as stops and beaters, and the story is told, and this was less than fifty years ago, of one ruler who, being displeased with his prime minister, tied him up as a 'kill'; and shot the tiger when it arrived.

What went on in those exalted circles bears little resemblance to what has been written in this book about the sport enjoyed by ordinary men, but they acted in all sincerity. It was all part of their way of life. And for those in whose honour these displays were staged there were advantages beyond those that immediately catch the eye. It rounds off the picture to consider them.

In the cold weather of 1921–2, the then Prince of Wales, the late Duke of Windsor, made a tour of India. He arrived in Bombay in *H.M.S. Renown* on November 17th and sailed from Karachi on March 17th. A fortnight was devoted to a trip to Burma, and of the remaining fifteen weeks about half was spent in visits to Indian States: and their rulers vied with one another to entertain him. After spending a week in Government House in Bombay he is alleged to have said that at last he realised how royalty lived, but nowhere was he more royally treated than by some of the more important princes.

Early in the tour he went to Udaipur, city of lakes and palaces, the most beautiful place in India. Its ruler, the Maharanah, the proudest member of the proudest family in India, greeted his guest with a fantastic display. Ellison compiled a record of the trip.

> 'In one night's run we seemed to have gone back two centuries. It would be difficult to imagine anything more gorgeously barbaric than the scenes; the astounding uniforms of the troops; men in coats of mail; men armed with long spears, others with immense old-fashioned muskets with inlaid butts and barrels two yards long; the wild Bhil horsemen; the painted elephants and a whole menagerie of beasts—leopard and bear and cheetah and fighting ram—chained on carts drawn up by the roadside.'

In Baroda the Prince saw gold and silver guns, and in the parade rode with the Gaekwar on his own elephant which was

> 'all yellow, the whole beast, body and legs and trunk and tail, all bright sulphur yellow. Its trappings were cloth of gold, and its howdah was gold; it wore great golden bosses on its tusks, and heavy anklets of twisted gold. It was painted in rich arabesque and, on each side of its head, reaching from the neck across the great cheeks, was painted a tiger rampant, black stripes on the yellow background; and where the painted tiger's eye was, there was the elephant's eye, even the lashes were yellow.'

In Gwalior each elephant had its own retinue and appeared in the order of battle under its own name.

A Battery of Horse Artillery.
The Elephant 'Shah Jehan'.
The Imperial Service Lancers.
A Troop of His Highness' Bodyguard.
The Elephant 'Moti Lal'.

They knew all about it, their place, the honour due to them and their rights of precedence; they needed no court chamberlain to remind them.

It may be asked what all this has to do with sport. The significance is that as soon as the panoply of state had been laid aside the rest of the time, apart perhaps from a banquet, was devoted to sport, and within the limits of the natural resources of each state no effort or expense was spared to ensure that the bag was as large and as representative as possible: there had been weeks, if not months, of preparation, directed in many cases by the ruler in person.

The royal visitor spent eight shooting days in the Terai jungles of Nepal. There had been some consternation because only five months' notice was given, it had been a year when his father was in India as King Emperor in 1911, but there were few signs of hasty improvisation. If a tiger coughed or a rhino settled for his sleep in the noonday heat, the news was flashed to a report centre at the main camp, over a network of telephone lines erected by a party of signallers lent by the army for the occasion. In order that the requisite number should be immediately available in whatever area it was decided to shoot, a total of 423 elephants were employed. The Prince's personal bag included two tigers and two rhinoceros, but many more were shot by members of his staff, who made up parties when he did not want to go out. On leaving he was presented with a collection large enough to start a small zoo. Twenty-eight animals, including a baby elephant and a rhino calf, and thirty-two birds.

On his visit to Gwalior he shot three tigers. He was stationed on a promontory of rocky cliff overlooking the deep nullah up which the game was driven. In Patiala a shoot had been arranged in which his staff shot a total bag of 254, mostly small game, but including two panthers. The Prince was otherwise engaged. In his early days his ruling passion was the horse, and he had a marked preference for any sport that could be pursued in or from the saddle. In Jodhpur he had been introduced to pigsticking so when the Maharajah of Patiala offered him this alternative to a formal shoot there was no doubt which he would choose. He killed two large boar.

Arrangements made in honour of the eldest son of the King Emperor were in a class of their own, but they differed only in degree from the occasions when shoots were organised for a viceroy or a provincial governor. There were sometimes dark rumours of the methods employed to ensure that the tiger, or whatever game it might be, duly presented itself to be shot by the guest of honour; on the other hand when perhaps no more than one day in a crowded programme could be set aside for sport, it was a sad anti-climax if that day was blank. And, anyway, a prince had to consider his reputation with his peers. Another *sine qua non* was that the honoured guest must be housed and fed in the utmost comfort, and on no account expected to exert himself physically in any way. Special camps, and even shooting boxes, would be erected, and the requisite number of Rolls Royces waiting to drive the party, over corduroy roads built through the jungle, to their machans, each the size of a ship's cabin, and suitably provided with refreshing drinks.

Apart from these state occasions many of the princes were keen sportsmen in their own right. The Maharajah Scindia of Gwalior, at the time of the Prince of Wales's visit, had shot over seven hundred tigers and was the author of a small handbook, *A Guide to Tiger Shooting*, which dealt in meticulous detail with the organisation of a large shoot. It included a few notes on omens, propitious and otherwise. 'It is considered inauspicious to meet a one-eyed man at the start of the day.' Have patch, cannot travel.

The duck shoots at Bharatpur have been mentioned in Chapter 16. The Maharajah would be there in person, dressed in a dove grey bush shirt, adorned with diamond solitaire buttons. The body of his large American car was made of burnished copper. 'I like to go around flashing like the setting sun'. It was upholstered with panther skins, and the horn played soft music. But the success of the shoots owed much to the fact that he was there in person to supervise them.

When Lord Hardinge, as Viceroy, on a visit to Kashmir, reached the camp from which he was to shoot barasingh, he found a thousand beaters assembled. The old Maharajah, prevented by age from taking an active part, turned up in a carriage and pair to see that all went well, and just could not understand his guest's preference to shoot his stag by stalking.

And what about those for whom all this trouble was taken? Odd though it may seem, viceroys and governors were human. Why should they not have a chance to shoot a tiger? They lived much in the public eye, their days heavy with responsibility. They were surrounded by insincerity and ceremonial for which many had little liking. If the bow was never unbent the strain would have been intolerable, and many have left it on record that it was only these escapes into the open air that kept them sane. And there were attendant advantages. In comparatively informal surroundings they could often discuss and settle with their host some problem that had defied the official approach. Above all, it was an opportunity to see, and be seen, by the people, the great masses whose uneventful lives were cheered by a splash of colour. The Indian of the countryside had a great regard for authority and it was all to the good that he should have the chance of seeing the great ones of the land and paying them his respects.

Lord Lytton, when Governor of Bengal, found relaxation in fishing in the rivers below Darjeeling, the hot weather seat of the Presidency government. He records an occasion when he started from a forest bungalow to ride the last three miles down to the stream. It was hot and he had changed into a pair of shorts and a flannel shirt. On arrival he was greeted by a very strange assemblage. The whole village had turned out to greet him.

> 'Triumphal arches decorated with greenery and wild flowers were erected over the road. Wild flowers in this part of the world were not buttercups and daisies, but plants which with us are found only in hothouses—hibiscus, daturas and orchids. A local band of half-naked villagers with tom-toms and strangely shaped wind pipes escorted us through the village and down to the river bank. A few local warriors who had been to France in the war were lined up for inspection. The local priest rang the bell of the local temple. And the object of all this homage and ceremony was a very unceremonious Governor, in shirt and shorts, with bare legs and arms for a holiday with his fishing rod and butterfly net.
>
> 'The procession conducted us to the water's edge, where a tent had been erected so that I could put up my rod screened from the rays of the sun, with a wicker stool covered with yellow silk for me to sit on, and a table covered with red silk bearing glasses and bottles of lemonade and ginger-ale for me to quench my thirst. Villagers stood round with various baits, fish, worms and grasshoppers. When we had completed all our preparations we stepped forward to the water's edge, while the local experts stepped back to a respectful distance, and the rest of the population gathered on the bridge and the surrounding hills to watch us.'

They had not much to offer, but what they had they gave.

# 18. The Hunter is Home

If the reader of this book thinks that all this shooting did any permanent damage to the wild life of India, taking the broad view of the matter, he is greatly mistaken. Many of the mighty Nimrods shot to excess, but even in their days as much and more damage was being done by local poachers, as firearms came into more general use. When the game laws were introduced about the 1880s they were enforced quite impartially on sportsman and poacher alike. The quota you were allowed to shoot on your game license was calculated by the forest officer on the basis of what he knew—and it was his business to know—his district would stand without the danger of any species being shot out.

It might be thought that once those allegedly blood-thirsty British officers had returned to the land from which they came the head of game of all sorts would increase; but this is not what has happened. There were an estimated 70,000 tigers in India in 1947. In a television programme on B.B.C. 2, *The Twilight of the Tiger*, the number of tigers surviving today is put at around 2,000, and the World Wild Life Organisation is mounting a campaign to save the species from extinction. The figures for other jungle animals show the same sad decrease. Philip Wayre, who filmed the programme which shows some remarkable shots of tigers, was told that there are now so many people to be housed and fed that it is difficult for the politician to justify the retention of even the smallest wild life sanctuaries. There is some truth in the claim, but it is not the whole truth. It is not the increase in the population so much as the increase in the number of firearms, on licenses granted for the supposed purpose of crop protection.

M. M. Ismail, writing in 1964 in *Call of the Tiger*, tells us that he was army representative on the board of wild life preservation of a state, but that he resigned after a few formal meetings when it became clear that the object was no more than to produce something on paper, and that neither the means nor the will existed to enforce the resolutions that were passed. The laws were there already, no further resolutions were needed. He forecasts that in less than thirty years:

> 'Our jungles will become silent except for the "chuckoo-chuckoo-chuckoo" of the nightjar, the sound of the insects and the whispering of the breeze in the tree tops. The girlish yelp of the cheetal doe, the awesome call of the tiger, the weird sawing

of the leopard and the metallic honk of the sambhur will be heard no more: things of enchanting beauty destroyed by the cruel hand of man.'

It is hoped that for some this book will have stirred up nostalgic memories: they can count themselves lucky to possess them. And if there is any doubt about the nature of those memories, here to convince the sceptics, is what three men have put on record. The last is written by the officer whose rifle got so hot beating off the Italian counter-attack at Sidi Barrani.

'In the hall and library are skins and heads as well as the old rifle that was my companion for so many years; and on the shelf repose the maps, old and stained with the canvas patched, which I had intended to hang upon the wall, but the days that are no more would arise with such poignant memories that they are better hidden away.'

Brigadier R. G. Burton—*Sport and Wild Life in the Deccan*:

'My memories of my service in India are not of politics or of administrative achievement or failure, but of the rush of the mighty mahseer in a mountain torrent, the whirr of rising duck on a Rajputana lake on a cold weather morning, a high partridge in the clear blue on the Wamkotal, a good horse under me, the smell of wood fire in camp in the evening, and dear friends.'

Sir Ronald Wingate (late I.C.S.) *Not in the Limelight*:

'And now when I climb up to the attic and see my tiger, bear and panther heads I feel apologetic and remember with relief that the last tigress I saw and could have shot in Balaghat I allowed to go unscathed.

'I have sent a subscription to the Greater Bustard Immigration Fund at Salisbury to atone for the houbaras I shot on the Indus.

'But I don't regret my Itis. After all, they all but got me for good at Keren.'

# Glossary

| | |
|---|---|
| Bagh | Clump of trees, orchard |
| Barasingh | A stag, lit: twelve-pointer |
| Bund | Built-up bank between fields |
| Chukor | Hill partridge |
| Chuppatti | Thin round bread cooked on griddle |
| Daffadar | Sergeant (mounted troops) |
| Houbara | The lesser bustard |
| Howdah | Elephant saddle |
| Jemadar | Indian officer—subaltern |
| Jheel | Lake |
| Jhow | Tamarisk |
| Khol | Glade |
| Khud | Steep hillside |
| Kitcharee | A rice dish |
| Machan | Platform from which to shoot, usually in a tree |
| Mahout | Elephant driver |
| Maidan | Open plain |
| Mohwa | Tree with rich blossom |
| Mugger | Crocodile |
| Nawab | Wealthy Mohamedan land owner |
| Nullah | Valley, ravine |
| Numdah | Felt |
| Rukh | Game preserve |
| Shikara | Kashmiri boat |
| Tonga | Horse drawn vehicle with two wheels |
| Zemindar | Landowner |

# Bibliography

(*—Outstanding books)


Allen, Hugh — *The Lonely Tiger*, Faber & Faber, 1960

Anderson, K. — *The Tiger Roars*, Allen & Unwin, 1967

Baden-Powell, Lord — *Pig-sticking or Hog-hunting*, Herbert Jenkins, c. 1928

Baker, — *Sport in Bengal*, Ledger, Smith & Co., 1887

Baker, Stuart — * *Game Birds of India, Burma and Ceylon*, Bombay Nat. Hist. Soc., 1921

Baldwin, — *Large and Small Game of Bengal*, H. S. King & Co., 1876

Best, Hon. J. W. — *Tiger Days*, John Murray, 1931

,, ,, ,, — *Shikar Notes for Novices*, Pioneer Press, 1921

Burrard, G. — * *Big Game Hunting in the Himalayas and Tibet*, H. Jenkins, 1926

Burton, R. G. — *Sport and Wild Life in the Deccan*, Seeley, Service & Co., 1928

Campbell, W. — *The Old Forest Ranger*, A. Hall, Virtue & Co., 1853

Corbett, Jim — * *Maneaters of Kumaon*, Oxford University Press, 1946

,, ,, — * *The Temple Tiger*, Oxford University Press, 1954

Dunbar-Brander, A. A. — * *Wild Animals in Central India*, E. Arnold & Co., 1923

Ellison, B. C. — *H.R.H. Prince of Wales's Sport in India*, Heinemann, 1925

Fayrer, J. — *The Royal Tiger of Bengal*, J. & A. Churchill, 1875

Forsyth, J. — * *The Highlands of Central India*, Chapman & Hall, 1889

Glasfurd, A. I. R. — *Leaves from an Indian Jungle*, The Times Press, Bombay, 1903

Gouldsbury, C. E. — *Tiger Slayer by Order*, Chapman & Hall, 1916

Handley, L. — *Hunter's Moon*, Macmillan & Co., 1927

Haughton, H. L. — *Sport & Folklore in the Himalayas*, E. Arnold & Co., 1913

Hume, A.
Marshall, C. H. T. — * *Game Birds of India, Burmah & Ceylon*, Author, 1881

Inglis, J. — *Sport & Work on the Nepaul Frontier*, Macmillan, 1872

Ismail, M. M. — *Call of the Tiger*, Faber & Faber, 1964

Kennion, B. L. — *Sport & Life in the Further Himalayas*, Blackwood, 1910

## BIBLIOGRAPHY


| | |
|---|---|
| Kinloch. A. A. | * *Large Game Shooting in Thibet and the North West*, Harrison, 1869 |
| Lytton, Earl of | *Pundits and Elephants*, Peter Davies, 1942 |
| Macdonald, A. StJ. | * *Circumventing the Mahseer*, Bombay Nat. Hist. Soc., c. 1935 |
| Pester, J. | * *War and Sport in India*, Heath, Cranton & Ouseley, 1913 |
| Powell, A. N. W. | *The Call of the Tiger*, Robert Hale, 1957 |
| Ronaldshay, Earl of | *Sport and Politics under an Eastern Sky*, Blackwood, 1902 |
| Sanderson, G. P. | * *Thirteen Years Among the Wild Beasts of India*, Allen, 1879 |
| Sher Jung | *Tryst with Tigers*, Robert Hale, 1967 |
| Skene Dhu | *The Mighty Mahseer*, Higginbotham, Madras, 1906 |
| Stebbing, E. P. | *Stalks in the Himalayas*, John Lane, 1912 |
| Sterndale, R. A. | * *Seonee*, Thacker, Spink & Co., Calcutta, 1887 |
| Stone, S. J. | *In and Beyond the Himalayas*, E. Arnold, 1896 |
| Taylor, N. | *Ibex Shooting on the Himalayas*, Sampson, Low & Marston, 1903 |
| Thomas, H. S. | *The Rod in India*, Stolz, Mangalore, 1873 |
| Tyacke, Mrs | *How I Shot my Bears*, Sampson, Low & Marston, 1893 |
| Various, | *The Hog Hunter's Annual*, Ed. Brig. J. Scott-Cockburn, 1928 onwards |
| Wardrop, A. E. | * *Modern Pigsticking*, Macmillan, 1914 |
| Wilson, A. | *Trout Fishing in Kashmir*, Thacker & Spink, 1921 |
| Whistler, H. | *In the High Himalayas*, Witherby, 1924 |

# Index

## INDEX